A GREAT WEEKEND IN

# PRAGUE

# Prague,
## a magical place

As the wind from the West blows in, Prague is undergoing some quite dramatic changes. However, despite the influences of Western capitalism, it remains one of the jewels in the crown of what was once Eastern Europe, exerting a kind of fascination as an erstwhile forbidden city, now released from an oppressive regime. But Prague had a considerable life and history before the political events of the 20th century, and there is much to see, experience and learn about this legendary city.

Galleries, restaurants and bars have opened their doors and the shops look inviting with brightly lit windows and tempting goods to buy. Some may say that the city is in danger of losing some of its mystery as a result, but much of Prague's past and the shadows of its musicians, writers and poets still seem to haunt the streets. The city has

For some time the walls and buildings of Prague were obscured by scaffolding and construction sites. As this work is nearing completion, the city's true colours are being revealed. On Staroměstské náměstí (Old Town Square) you'll find an array of yellow, ochre, pink and grey buildings, all in perfect harmony. In many parts of the city, as building work is carried out

and façades are repainted, gradually the old grey leaden shadows of Prague are being chased away, and a softer, pastel city is emerging.

Despite the devastating floods of August 2002, you won't see much evidence of the damage the city suffered, and it is rare now to see closed doors or barred passageways as was the case until just a few years ago.

really changed very little and walking about, you feel as if you have just stepped onto the set of a period drama. Dip into a collection of stories about Prague and you'll find that tales of the ghosts and monsters abound, and according to folklore, the buildings and the river come alive at night. Take a stroll in the castle courtyard at dusk, or walk down to the Malá Strana (Little Quarter) and across Charles Bridge (Karlův most), lined with a silent guard of

honour of thirty statues along its ramparts. Continue your walk into the Staré Město (Old Town), where the bright colours of the buildings fade in the pale light of the street lamps, and narrow alleyways and passages cast their spells once more. It's a world where time has stood still. Climb the tower of the Powder Gate, one of the few remaining parts of the Old Town's fortifications, for a fabulous view over the rooftops, before making your way to a *hospoda* or tavern to sample one of the many beers for which Prague is renowned. If you're a night-owl, head for a jazz club or a nightclub. This is a great place for music

lovers and there are many opportunities to listen to live performances, with regular concerts and operas held all over the city. Mozart even dedicated one of his symphonies to Prague and there is a museum dedicated to him in the villa Betramka where he stayed several times on his visits here.

Prague is one of Europe's smallest and most magical capitals, but despite the new Western influences, you'll find that the city's rhythm is very different from the fever pitch at which most European cities run. It developed as four separate towns and a Jewish ghetto – Hradčany, Malá Strana (Little Quarter), Staré Město (Old Town), Nové Město (New Town) and Josefov (Jewish quarter). Their medieval street plans remain largely intact, and it's here that you'll find most of the city's historical buildings and sites.

The heart of the city is the Staré Město (Old Town) with its stunning square and astronomical clock on the Old Town Hall, always a great favourite with visitors. You can spend many happy hours around here, wandering through the quieter backstreets and narrow alleyways.

If you want to explore further afield, the transport system is easy to master, efficient and excellent value. You can escape the crowds on Petřín Hill or in Vyšehrad, with views across the river towards Prague Castle which has been a part of the city's skyline for over 1,000 years.

Prague has a great deal to offer the visitor. Small and compact, it is full of history and mystery, so relax, soak up the atmosphere and enjoy your weekend in Prague.

# How to get there

Prague is a beautiful city at all times of the year, but temperatures and numbers of tourists do differ with the seasons. Here are a few suggestions on what to expect when you visit Prague and how to get there.

## THE CLIMATE

A flood of tourists descends on Prague from June to the end of August. Temperatures are pleasant and warm enough for the cafés to open up their terraces, but beware the possibility of sudden, sometimes violent, downpours. In the winter months, from October to March, the weather is cold and dry, sometimes sunny but mostly overcast. Temperatures can fall as low as -20°C (-4°F). If you're lucky enough to be in Prague after a snowfall, you'll see it take on a new and different kind of magic. You may even find you have the Charles Bridge to yourself. In the winter it gets dark at around 4pm, making days rather short. Spring and autumn are pleasant times of year to visit and there are fewer tourists.

## GETTING THERE

For a great weekend in Prague, flying is the best option. Many airlines offer direct flights and you can call direct, book online or ask your travel agent.

## FLIGHTS FROM THE UK

**British Airways**
www.british-airways.com
☎ 0845 77 333 77
Offers daily flights to Prague.

**Easyjet**
www.easyjet.com
☎ 0870 60 000 00
Daily flights from London Stansted.

**ČSA (Czechoslovak Airlines)**
www.csa.cz ☎ 020 7255 1898
Regular flights from London Heathrow and Stansted.

## SHORT BREAKS

Travel agencies often offer short-break package trips to Prague which are good value for money, offering flight and accomodation in one package. Ask at your local travel agency or check on the internet – try:
www.talkingcities.co.uk
or www.enroute.co.uk
Both offer all-inclusive weekend breaks.

## CHEAP FLIGHTS

Try looking on the internet for cheap flights – the following websites often have good deals:
www.opodo.co.uk
www.expedia.msn.com
www.deckchair.com
www.ebookers.com
Easyjet probably offer the cheapest deals (from as little as £23 return), but prices rise as the flights fill up, so book well in advance (see p. 4). Students under 26 looking for cheaper fares should contact their local branch of STA travel (www.sta-travel.com) or Council Travel (www.counciltravel.com).

## FROM IRELAND

**British Airways**
www.british-airways.com
☎ 1 800 626 747
Offers flights from Shannon, Cork and Dublin via London Heathrow.

## FROM THE USA AND CANADA

**ČSA (Czech Airlines)**
www.csa.cz
☎ 212 765 6022
Offers a code share agreement with Delta, Crossair/Swiss and Continental. There are flights from a number of US airports via major European cities, although some direct flights are available. Check the website or call for details.

**British Airways**
www.british-airways.com
☎ 1 800 AIRWAYS
Regular flights via London from all over the USA and Canada.

**Delta**
www.delta.com
☎ 1 800 241 4141
Regular flights via Zurich.

## FROM AUSTRALIA AND NEW ZEALAND

ČSA offers code share agreement with Qantas, but most of the major South Pacific airlines offer flights to Prague. From Australia you can fly with British Airways via London. From New Zealand you may have to change carrier en-route.

Check with your travel agent for flight details or try looking on the internet (see box on left).

## BY TRAIN

You can get the train to Prague from any major city in Europe. If you are travelling from the UK or Ireland it is not much cheaper (if at all) to go by train, and the journey takes about 15 hours. For information on routes and to book seats, contact Rail Europe on
☎ 08705 848 848.
www.raileurope.co.uk

International trains arrive at the main station (Hlavní nádraží).

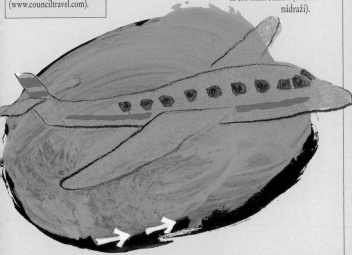

## BY BUS
### FROM THE UK
This is a reasonably cheap way to get to Prague from the UK (less than £100), and does not take any longer than the train. Eurolines (☎ 08705 143219) runs a regular service to Prague. Visit their website at: www.eurolines.co.uk for more information or ask at any major travel agency.

## FROM THE AIRPORT TO THE CITY CENTRE

### BY BUS
Prague's airport, Ruzyně (☎ 201 111 11) is situated 20 km/12 miles west of the city. There's no metro station at the airport, so the easiest way to get to the city centre is by 119 bus, which terminates at Dejvická metro station (green line A). There's an automatic ticket machine in the arrivals area. If you change money at the airport, make sure you have enough change for the ticket (Kč12). The journey takes approximately 30 minutes. At Dejvická you can join the metro. Hold onto your bus ticket as you will be able to continue using it on the metro. The basic Kč12 ticket allows you to use any mode of transport (bus, metro, tram) and make any number of changes within a 90 min period (60 mins 5am-8pm weekdays).

### BY MINIBUS
ČSA (Czechoslovak Airlines) runs a bus service carrying a maximum of 6 passengers

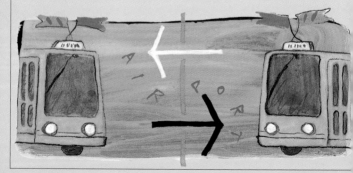

and will take you to Dejvická or to the centre, stopping at Náměstí Republiky (yellow line B). The bus leaves every 30 minutes or when the minibus is full. The journey takes 20 minutes and you can buy your ticket on the bus (Kč90).

## BY TAXI

You can take an 'airport taxi' to the city centre (ie one of the white Mercedes that have a monpoly on taxis leaving the airport), but the ride will cost you Kč500–1000 plus…! It's better to call AAA (☎ 1080) or Profi (☎ 1035); both firms speak English. They will collect you from near the billboards to the right of the airport terminal exit and charge roughly Kč350 to the centre. A minibus will cost Kč395 per person.

## FORMALITIES

EU citizens, Americans and Canadians can all travel to Prague without a visa as long as they are planning to stay less than 180 days, after this 180-day period a visa is necessary. You must also ensure that your passport is valid before you go.

Citizens of New Zealand can travel to Prague without a visa if they intend to stay less than 90 days. Australian citizens require a tourist visa valid for up to 30 days, which should be obtained from your embassy at home before departing (see p. 9 for addresses). You can also obtain a multiple-entry 90 day visa.

## CUSTOMS

Entering the Czech Republic, personal goods are not subject to customs duty. The duty free allowance is two litres of wine, one litre of spirits and 200 cigarettes or 200gm/7oz tobacco. Customs require an export licence for expensive goods such as antiques.

For more information on antiques, contact the **Museum of Decorative Arts** (Uměleckoprůmyslové) at Ul.17. listopadu 2, Prague 1, ☎ 51 09 31 11.

For paintings and statues, contact the **National Gallery** (Sternberg Palace) at Hradčanské náměstí, 15, Prague 1, ☎ 20 51 46 34.

(see p. 9 for addresses)

## PUBLIC HOLIDAYS

New Year's Day (1 Jan.); Easter Monday; Labour Day (1 May); VE Day (8 May); Remembrance of the Slavonic Missionaries (5 July); Anniversary of death of Jan Hus in 1415 (6 July); Foundation of the Republic in 1918 (28 Oct.); Christmas Eve, Christmas Day and Boxing Day.

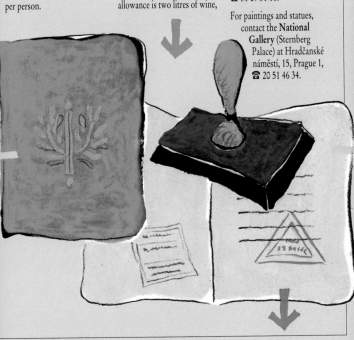

For information on exporting coins, contact the **National Museum** (Národní Muzeum) at Václavské náměstí, 68, ☎ 24 49 71 11.

## BUDGET

You'll have to allow quite a large budget for your accommodation. Hotels are very expensive in Prague, just as they are in any other European capital. The average price for a category B hotel is around Kč1,500 per night. On the other hand, eating local dishes in the *hospodas* will cost you around Kč125.

You'll be able to go to a theatre, nightclub or concert without going bankrupt as ticket prices and drinks are generally reasonably priced.

## LOCAL CURRENCY

The local currency is the Czech koruna (Kč). Notes come in denominations of Kč20, Kč50, Kč100, Kč200, Kč500, Kč1,000, Kč2,000 and Kč5,000. Coins come in denominations of Kč1, Kč2, Kč5, Kč10, Kč20 and Kč50, and 10, 20 and 50 halérů (h) or hellers and 100 hellers = 1 koruna. You may find it difficult to change a Kč500 note in some shops, so keep smaller denominations on you.

It's now legal to bring Czech currency in and out of the country but it's probably best to buy your crowns once you get there and use them up before returning home. Don't forget that you can use your credit cards and bank cards in the ATMs and this might be a more practical way to get hold of Czech money. The Czech Republic is working towards membership of the European Union, after which the euro will no doubt be introduced. Hotels and tour operators in the Czech Republic are already quoting prices in euros for international bookings.

## HEALTH CARE

You don't need any vaccinations to go to the Czech Republic but you are advised to take out comprehensive medical insurance.

## RELIGIOUS SERVICES

Every Sunday at 11am St Thomas's Church (Kostel

### ISIC CARDS

Students and others under 26 should obtain an ISIC Card (International Student Identity Card) which get you discounts on transport, museum entry and shows. You should be able to obtain one from specialist student travel agencies, such as STA or Council Travel.

sv. Tomáše) has a Catholic Church service conducted in English. Malá Strana, Prague 1.

St Clement's Church (Koste sv. Klimenta) offers a Church of England service in English at 11am on Sunday. Klimentská 18, Prague 1.

## LOCAL TIME

Prague is on Central European Time (GMT plus one hour) except from the end of March to the end of September, when Summer Time takes effect (GMT plus two hours).

## PACKING YOUR SUITCASE

If you're visiting Prague in the summer, just pack normal light clothing. Don't forget to pack a pair of comfortable walking shoes. This is a city to explore on foot, and the cobbled streets can be very uneven.

If you are visiting in winter, take a hat, a scarf, a warm coat and waterproof shoes. It can get *very* cold! The cafés, restaurants and hotel rooms are often overheated, so wear layers of clothes you can peel off easily.

Whatever the season, remember to pack a smart outfit for a visit to the opera or to a classical concert. When it snows in the winter, carry your evening shoes in a bag and put them on in the cloakroom on arrival – this is what the locals do.

## LANGUAGE

Czech is the national language, but you'll find that English and German are often understood, which is helpful as Czech is

not the easiest language to understand or speak! Handy words and phrases in Czech can be found on the back flap of the cover and on page 121.

## VOLTAGE

The electrical supply is 220 volts, as in the rest of Europe, and Czech plugs have two pins. Bring an adaptor with you for British and US plugs.

### CZECH EMBASSIES

#### UK AND IRELAND
Czech Embassy
26 Kensington Palace
Gardens, London W8 4QY
☎ 020 7243 1115
website:
www.czechembassy.org.uk

#### USA
Czech Embassy
3900 Spring of Freedom St
NW, Washington DC 20008
☎ 202 966 8540
e-mail:
washington@embassy.mzv.cz

#### CANADA
Czech Embassy
541 Sussex Drive, Ottawa
Ontario, K1N 6Z6
☎ 613 562 3875

#### AUSTRALIA
Czech Embassy
38 Culgoa Circuit
O'Malley, Canberra
ACT 2606
☎ 02 6290 1386

#### NEW ZEALAND
Czech Consulate
48 Hair Street,
PO Box 43035
Wainuiomata
Wellington
☎ 04 564 6001

For embassies and consulates in Prague, see page 33.

# THE GREAT MUSICAL TRADITION

You'll be surrounded by music wherever you go in Prague – it's an integral part of the Czech character. You'll hear it in churches, most of which are now concert halls, in gardens during the summer months, on Charles Bridge and in the Old Town Square. You'll never be far from a performance of a sonata or requiem, and you'll soon appreciate the local saying that there's a musician lurking inside every Czech citizen.

## EUROPE'S CONSERVATOIRE OF MUSIC

The English composer Charles Burney was so impressed in 1772 by the knowledge and technical skill of the musicians he met in Prague that he called the city the 'conservatoire of Europe'. This turned out to be a premonition – the first conservatoire subsequently opened its doors here in 1811. The Museum of Musical Instruments, which houses 3,000 pieces, is another testimony to just how musical the city is. Located at Lázeňská 2, call for opening times, ☎ 53 08 43.

## NATIONAL TREASURES

The musician Bedřich Smetana (1824-1884) did most to put

*Antonín Dvořák, head of the Prague Conservatoire (1901)*

the Czech national identity on the musical map. He was the first composer to integrate popular songs and dances into his classical works, of which the most famous are *The Bartered Bride* and *My Fatherland*. This tradition was continued by Antonín Dvořák (1841-1904), the famous composer of the *New World Symphony*, Leoš Janáček (1854-1928) and Bohuslav Martinů (1890-1959).

## MOZART, FREEMAN OF PRAGUE

Prague has a strong tradition of celebrating not just its own

*Bedřich Smetana, founder of Czezh opera*

national geniuses but also those of foreign countries, such as Beethoven, Liszt, Chopin, Berlioz and Mozart. An Austrian tired of being misunderstood by his Viennese public, Mozart decided to give

*Wolfgang Amadeus Mozart (1756-1791)*

the first performance of *The Marriage of Figaro* in Prague. A warm welcome awaited him, and he was so overwhelmed by the ovation that he made his famous announcement: 'My fellow citizens of Prague understand me.' The much-loved Mozart came to Prague only four times, but the Mozart museum is here, located in Betramka,

Mozartova, 169, and is open every day 9.30am-6pm. Mozart stayed here with the family of his friend and composer Dušek while working on *Don Giovanni*.

## PRAGUE SPRING MUSIC FESTIVAL

Established in 1946, this prestigious festival opens annually on 12 May, the anniversary of the death of Bedřich Smetana. After the ritual mass has taken place at his grave, his great symphony *My Fatherland* is played in the Municipal House (Obecní Dům), in the room named after him. Beethoven's Ninth Symphony closes the event on 3 June.

## THE CZECH PHILHARMONIC ORCHESTRA

Václav Talich, Rafael Kubelík and Karel Ancerl are among the famous conductors who have contributed to the orchestra's reputation, and Antonín

Dvořák himself conducted the first concert on 4 January 1896. Unfortunately, Gerd Albrecht, the German conductor appointed in 1992, had to relinquish his post in 1995 due to 'nationalist' pressures. Ironically enough, he was promptly replaced by a Russian, Vladimír Ashkenazy. There are two other official orchestras, the Prague Symphony and the radio orchestra. However, there are also dozens of other unofficial ones, including several chamber music groups. Quatuor Talich deserves a mention, being amongst the best of these.

*Karel Špillar's Homage to Prague on the Municipal House façade. The arts are represented, with 'Music' shown on the right.*

# PRAGUE, QUEEN OF BAROQUE

Neo-Baroque building in the Old Town, built at the beginning of the century

You'll come across Baroque architecture all over Prague. There are exotic churches, grand palaces and more statues than you could possibly count. The great paradox is that Baroque architecture was something that was imposed on Prague, as a weapon in the fight against Protestantism. However, the city managed to integrate this architectural style successfully, and it eventually became an expression of the Czech national spirit.

### HOW BAROQUE ART CAME TO PRAGUE

The defeat at the Battle of the White Mountain in 1621 made Bohemia a province of Austria. Under the Catholic Habsburg rule Prague was totally reshaped. The citizens of Prague saw the Reformation as an attack on their city which was demonstrated very graphically by the construction of the Klementinum by the Jesuits who destroyed 32 houses, two gardens, three churches and a

Dominican convent to make space for it. The intellectual élite was banished, and Prague fell under the dark Baroque influence, which was used as a weapon of war against the former religion.

### ARTISTIC INFLUENCES

Two strong artistic influences came together in Prague. The marriage between the classical style from Austria and France and a Baroque style of Italian and German origins, took

place between 1700-1740 against the perfect backdrop of the city, with its wonderfully appropriate dramatic terrain.

### BRAUN AND BROKOF

There are more statues in Prague than in any other city in the world. They're on the façades of homes and churches and in the squares, and are the city's most

Church of St Nicholas in Old Town Square

characteristic Baroque feature. Many of them were the inspiration of two key figures, Mathias Bernard Braun and Ferdinand Maximilien Brokof. Braun and Brokof were contemporaries, born in 1684 and 1688 respectively, and they both died of lung disease caused by their years of stone cutting. Don't miss the statue of Saint Luitgard on Charles Bridge, the twelfth statue on the right starting from the Old Town. Sculpted by Braun in 1710, it's a voluptuous pastiche of Bernini. In the following year Brokof sculpted the statue of St Frances Xavier, fifth on the left.

## LIKE FATHER, LIKE SON

Kristof Dientzenhofer (1655-1722) came from a family of Bavarian masons, and, together with his son Kilian

Ignaz (1689-1751) and the latter's son-in-law, Anselmo Lurago, they gave the Czech capital its most beautiful Baroque buildings. They were responsible for the façades of the Loreto and the Church of St Nicholas in the Old Town (not to be confused with the Church of St Nicholas in the Little Quarter, the magnificent creation of the same dynasty).

*The Loreto*

## WHERE TO FIND BAROQUE ARCHITECTURE IN PRAGUE

You won't have to go far to discover the Baroque in Prague. You'll see grand palaces, smaller houses and statues on churches, all Baroque in style. If you wander around the

Malá Strana (Little Quarter) and Staré Město (Old Town), you will come across many Baroque buildings. Not to be missed are the following: Klementinum (see p. 58), St Nicholas's in the Staré Město (see p. 48), Loreto (see p. 34), Buquoy Palace (see p. 50), Wallenstein Palace (see p. 50), Charles Bridge (see p. 46), Nerudova Street (see p. 49) and Villa Amerika (see p. 41).

## A NEO-BAROQUE DESIGNER

Bořek Šípek takes you back to the Baroque era with his padded armchairs, straight from the time of Mozart, and his extravagant coloured glass vases. He was exiled to Germany in 1968, and then to Holland in 1983, finally returning to Prague after the Velvet Revolution in 1989. Since 1992, he has been in charge of the reconstruction of Prague Castle. Šípek is an accomplished and eclectic artist, who has been responsible for the refurbishment of Karl Lagerfeld's shops all over the world, together with the design of the first porcelain table service to be commissioned by the Sèvres manufacturers since the 18th century.

*Detail of Alfons Mucha window in St Vitus's Cathedral*

# PRAGUE IN 1900 – SECESSION AND CUBISM

At the turn of the 19th and 20th centuries, an overwhelming explosion of creativity launched Prague to the forefront of European art. The Czech Secession movement has its origins in Germany's Jugendstil, Austria's own Secession and France's Art Nouveau. There are over three hundred Art Nouveau-style buildings in the city. Above all, don't miss the Europa Café.

## ART NOUVEAU

First displayed at the Jubilee Exhibition in 1891, Art Nouveau is characterised by its curved sinuous lines and its floral motifs. It was a reaction against the academic establishment.

## A TOTAL ART FORM

Art Nouveau became a total art form and influenced not only architecture and painting but also decorative arts.

Stained-glass windows, wallpaper, mosaics, furniture and jewellery were all involved in what became not just an art form but a way of life.

## ALFONS MUCHA, ART NOUVEAU ARTIST

Alfons Mucha, born in 1860 in Moravia, is the most famous Czech artist and one of the most successful exponents of the Art Nouveau style. The natural world was the inspiration for his exotic figures with their flowing hair, often set against floral backgrounds with tentacle-like forms. It was in Paris in 1894 that Mucha became famous through a poster designed for Sarah Bernhardt. A painter, illustrator, sculptor and creator of stylised clothes and jewellery, he was turned down by the Academy and left Prague at the age of 19. He returned to live in the city in 1910, and was commissioned to decorate the Mayor's room in the Municipal House. Don't miss the Mucha Museum (Panská, 7, ☎ 22 42 16 415 www.mucha.cz), which is open every day 10am-6pm.

The museum shop has some wonderful Mucha-inspired gifts and art books.

## A GREAT PLACE TO SHOP

At Melantrichova, 5, **Art Décoratif** is well worth a visit. Here you will find wonderful copies of Art Nouveau items, some of them made by Alfons Mucha's own granddaughter. There's a huge selection of Art Nouveau lamps and replicas of Mucha's jewellery, such as the butterfly brooch designed for Sarah Bernhardt. An Art Deco set of six glasses and a decanter will cost around Kč3,600. A limited series vase will set you back Kč12,000, and for the superb replicas of the wall lamps designed for the Municipal House you will pay as much as Kč41,000. Open every day 10am-8pm, ☎ 26 08 34.

## BABA VILLAS

The small Baba district is a little out of the way but well worth the trip. There are 33 villas, built between 1928-1933 by members of the Czech architectural avant-garde (including Josef Gočár and Adolf Loos), and conceived as a 'Constructivist colony' by Pavel Janák, born-again functionalist. Take tram 20 or 25 to the area and look out for the following streets: Na ostrohu, Na Babě, Nad Pat'ankou, Jarní and Průhledová. Unfortunately, the houses aren't open to the public, so you'll have to content yourself with their external architecture only. Some of the houses have been altered but others remain just as they were originally.

## CUBISM

From 1910 onwards, Prague gave in to the Cubist influence, which came about as a reaction to the soft, curved lines of the Art Nouveau style. Braque and Picasso were the founders of the movement. The group of 'Plastic Artists', as they were then called, took on the help of the architects Josef Chochol, Josef Gočár and Pavel Janák to work on Cubist buildings. These are located at the foot of the Vyšehrad (see p. 64).

(see p. 64)

(see p. 47)
(see p. 55)

## AN ART NOUVEAU DAY OUT

Having reached the main railway station (Wilsonova 8/300), you can enjoy breakfast at the **Europa Hotel**, gather your thoughts in front of the Jan Hus Monument, by Ladislav Šaloun, and then make your way to the **Mucha museum**. Have a spot of lunch at the **Pařίž Hotel** and dedicate your

afternoon to a visit of the **Museum of Decorative Arts** (see p. 47). In the evening go to a concert and then dinner at the **Municipal House (Obecní Dům)**. Finish your evening off with a nightcap at the **Lucerna Bar** (see p. 55), the perfect end to an 'Art Nouveau' day.

## KAFKA, HASEK AND HRABAL – PRAGUE'S GREAT FIGURES

Prague has been visited by and written about by many international authors, but it has its own literary giants, amongst them Hašek, Hrabal and, of course, Kafka. He is an extremely popular figure with tourists, and references

*Kinský Palace where Kafka was a student until 1901.*

to Kafka are everywhere in the city. His writing was influenced greatly by Prague, of which he said that it 'never lets go of you... this little mother has claws. We ought to set fire to it at both ends, on Vyšehrad and Hradčany, and maybe then it might be possible to escape'.

### FRANZ KAFKA

Born in Prague in 1883 into a Jewish family, Kafka is without doubt the most famous Czech author. A member of the German-speaking Jewish community, he wrote in German, and his works *The Trial* and *The Metamorphosis* are both internationally renowned. He spent the majority of his life around Josefov, the old Jewish quarter, but gradually the ghetto

*Franz Kafka was no stranger to solitude and in his writings created a world at the centre of which was the chasm between the individual and the world around him.*

disappeared and a new city emerged, in which he no longer felt at ease. 'The unhealthy old Jewish ghetto within us is more real that the new hygienic one that surrounds us', said Kafka, in 1902. He frequented literary salons, including the Café Louvre, the Savoy, the Café Arco and the Slavia, where he enjoyed spirited debates with intellectuals and artists. At Café Stefan the first reading of *The Metamorphosis* took place, presented by Ernst Pollack. Before Kafka died in 1924, he asked his friend Max Brod to burn all his work. Luckily, Brod disobeyed, and the majority of Kafka's work was published after his death.

## BOHUMIL HRABAL

Bohumil Hrabal was born in 1914, and in 1946 he became a doctor of Law, a career he did not pursue. Instead, his many career moves included railwayman, commercial traveller, steel factory worker, packer and theatre extra. He spent a good deal of his time watching,

## JAROSLAV HASEK

Hašek was Kafka's contemporary. Born in the same year, 1883, he wrote *The Good Soldier Švejk*. Writer, journalist, great orator, bigamist and People's Commissar in the Red Army, Hašek was a great humorist and one of Prague's colourful characters. He spent much of his time in taverns and bars, and was snubbed by the intellectual circles of Prague. Despite this, *The Good Soldier Švejk* became a highly popular play throughout Central Europe. Hašek died at the age of 40, and it was left to a friend to complete the last volume of the adventures of the naïve but artful soldier. His work is one of the greatest achievements of Czech literature, with its humour and its echoes of Don Quixote and Sancho Panza.

listening and writing. He had no real intention of being published and was inspired by human nature and conversations in bars. However, many of his works were indeed published from 1963 onwards, to critical and public acclaim. He became the most successful Czech author of the 1960s, with works including *Closely Observed Trains*, which was made into an equally brilliant film by Jiří Menzl. He wrote *The Little Town Where Time Stood Still*, *Dancing Lessons*, *Too Loud a Solitude* and *I Served the King of England*. His works combined poetry and comedy with a touch of Prague's idiosyncratic humour and a good dash of slang. His death on 3 February 1997 shocked the country, when he fell from the fifth floor

### IN KAFKA'S FOOTSTEPS

Make a quick pilgrimage to the Old Town Square (Staroměstské náměstí). Kafka was born in Maiselova, to the left of St Nicholas Church From 1893-1901, he studied

at Kinský Palace, the former German language imperial school, at no. 12 h on the square. The Kafka family lived in the house at no. 3 (Dům U Minuty), decorated with sgraffiti, and at Celetná 3, close to the Gothic church. Kafka's grave is in the new Jewish cemetery of Olšány (metro A, Želivského station).

of the Bulovka Hospital in Prague. If you want to know more about his world before embarking on his writings, enjoy a beer in the Golden Tiger tavern (see p. 59), where he spent much of his time.

# GLASS AND CRYSTAL

Bohemian glass has ranked amongst the finest in the world since the 14th century, rivalling its Venetian and Baccarat counterparts. It is made of a mixture of metal and Bohemian sand, and its exact composition is a secret closely guarded by the Czech master glass-makers. The only known fact is that they don't use lead.

## BOHEMIAN GLASS

Glass has been made in Bohemia since the Early Middle Ages. It was used on bracelets and necklaces, and it was blown to make glasses. You can see it in the lovely mosaic on the south portal of St Vitus's Cathedral. In the 16th century, the Habsburg court began demanding more sophisticated pieces, and the artists responded with

Renaissance-style objects, inspired by Venetian crystal. Towards 1600, Rudolph II's jeweller, Caspar Lehmann, experimented with a technique used only in precious stone engraving, involving bronze and copper wheels. Thanks to him, the art of engraving glass took off in Bohemia. Glasses with polished stems and Baroque designs and goblets made of finely cut glass engraved with floral motifs are now exported throughout the world.

## ACHIEVING PERFECTION

From 1720, glassworkers began to gild and paint their creations, which were soon more prized than those made in Venice. In the following century, the colour, detail and pattern all improved dramatically. Empire and Biedermeier styles became fashionable, resulting in finely shaped, engraved glass. Europe began to discover the East, and Count Georg Buquoy developed a technique of making thick, opaque glass, which he then embellished with Chinese motifs and encrusted with agate and rubies. Bohemian crystal became famous for its exquisite plates, glass jewellery and mirrors. In the 20th century, the designs came under the influence of Art Nouveau and Cubist styles, which resulted in some very avant-garde pieces. There was a wonderful sense of creativity in the air. Even today the pieces made during this period appear very bold and continue to inspire modern designers throughout the world.

*Visit the Museum of Czech Glass to see the master glass-makers at work in the basement in very high temperatures.*

## THE HISTORY OF LEAD

The customary method of making crystal includes lead. It is lead which makes the glass softer, easier to engrave and to cut. Its luminosity is increased as more lead is added. Some Czech master glass-workers continue to work without lead, as was the tradition in former times. The famous Moser glass-works is one such company.

They replace the lead with a complex chemical composition, which gives the glass clarity, quality and strength. In Prague, fine examples of leadfree glass can command prices as high as their French or English equivalents. Visit the **Moser** Shop at Na příkopĕ 12. ☎ 24 21 12 93 or Male náměstí, 11 ☎ 21 61 15 20 (see also pages 90 & 91)

## LEAD CONTENT IN CRYSTAL

The long term effects of lead on alcohol and the resulting risk to health have yet to be proven. It's advisable not to keep alcohol in a crystal decanter for too long as small particles may penetrate the liquid. According to the criteria set down by the European Union, glass contains less than 4% lead, crystal more than 10% and very high quality crystal at least 30%. Baccarat crystal from France contains 34%. In the Czech Republic real crystal has a lead content of at least 24%. Crystalline contains less lead but more barium oxide, which gives it the required colour and luminosity.

### MUSEUMS

**Museum of Decorative Arts (Umělecko-průmyslové muzeum/UPM)**
Ul. 17. listopadu 2, Prague 1
☎ 51 09 31 11
Open Tue.-Sun. 10am-6pm

This museum houses collections of furniture, posters, ceramics and porcelain, but that's not all. You'll be able to learn the art of Bohemian glass-making from the Middle Ages to the present day and see a stunning collection of Art Deco pieces.

**Museum of Czech Glass (Muzeum cěše ho sklq)**
Staroměstské náměstí, 26, Prague 1
☎ 24 23 80 51
Every day 10am-7pm (8pm in summer).

Once you've seen the 14th and 20th century collections, go down into the basement of this museum and see master glass-workers at their craft. It's wonderful to see the molten glass transformed into stunning crystal items, but be prepared for the high temperatures.

# PRAGUE'S PASSION FOR PUPPETS

Prague is a puppet paradise. You will find them everywhere, as popular and well-loved today as they were two hundred years ago. It's not surprising to learn that the international puppet society was established in Prague in 1929, raising the status of the puppet industry to that of an art form. The organisation now boasts more than 8000 members in a total of 77 countries.

## A FOREIGN IMPORT

What has now become a national passion for puppets was originally imported into Bohemia after the Thirty Years War (1618-1648), by English, German and Italian troupes. Towards the end of the 18th century, the Czechs began to make their own puppets, reinforcing their sense of national identity.

## THE GOLDEN AGE

At the turn of the 19th and 20th centuries, the puppet theatre underwent a 'renaissance' of its own. Artists and designers, such as the painters Vít Skála and Ota Bubeníček and the sculptor Ladislav Šaloun, confirmed it as a valid art form. In 1911, the 'Czech Union of Friends of the Puppet' was launched to be followed by the *Czech Puppet Magazine* in 1912. In the 1920s many hundreds of theatre societies and schools were formed, and the popularity of the puppet really took off.

## ALES' PUPPETS

The painter Mikuláš Aleš (1852-1913) was renowned for his frescoes, which were seen in many Prague homes. However, at the beginning of the 20th century he created his famous 'Aleš' Puppets'. His original intention was

merely to entertain his children with his naive cardboard figures and their oversized heads. His designs then became the model for the first mass produced Czech puppets. They came onto the market in 1912 and are still a commercial success. Look closely at the 'wise man with the white beard' puppet because this is a self-portrait of the artist himself.

## SPEJBL AND HURVINEK

The best known puppet show in the city is held at the Špejbl and Hurvínek theatre (Divadlo Špejbla a Hurvínka). Špejbl is the unrepentant father of Hurvínek, his reprobate son who has a falsetto voice. They are instantly recognisable with their huge rustic clogs and were conceived in the 1920s by Josef Skupa (1892-1957). They are now stars of the small screen, having been immortalised by the famous animated film-maker, Jiří Trnka.

## LITTLE GASPARD

In this puppet play there are twelve protagonists, made up of Guignol, the devil, Death, six male characters and three female ones. They vary in size and are all-string marionettes (ie not glove or rod.) Guignol, the Mr Punch figure, was adopted by the Czech public in 1810 and renamed 'Little Gaspard' or Kašpárek.

## THE PRAGUE NATIONAL MARIONETTE THEATRE

Created in 1911, this theatre played its part in the revival of the great Czech tradition of study and learning. The majority of the fifty members of the troupe hold diplomas in the art of puppet theatre from an academy of dramatic art. If you are a purist, you won't want to miss the most famous pieces in the repertory. *Don Giovanni* was written in 1782, five years before the opening of Mozart's opera in Prague. **For information and tickets:** Žatecká 1, ☎ 232 25 36.

## PUPPET SHOWS FOR CHILDREN

The **Children's Theatre** has a puppet show most days and the Children's Little Sun Club puts on the occasional show. **For information and tickets:** via Praga Vojtíškova 1783, ☎ 790 20 74. (also see p. 116 and 117).

(also see p. 116 and 117).

### POD LAMPOU PUPPET SHOP

**U Lužického semináře 5 Open every day 11am-8pm.**

In a tiny shop at the foot of the Charles Bridge, you will find wooden, ceramic and plaster puppets, all suspended from the ceiling. It opened in 1994 and is designed to look like a dolls' house. The owner, Pavel Truhlar, has enormous respect for the quality of the little figures he sells and only buys from hand-picked artists. Choose from over 1,500 models ranging in price from Kč190-17000.

# BOHEMIAN GARNETS

Bohemia is known for its semi-precious stones, and craftsmen have been working with garnets for many years. Garnet is extracted in the north of the Czech Republic, in Turnov, not far from Český Ráj, which means 'Czech paradise'. It remains one of the most sought-after stones.

## A SHORT HISTORY OF GARNET

Until the Middle Ages, garnet was used for medicinal purposes as well as being set as jewellery. At the end of the 16th century, it became fashionable to set the stone in rings, as was the practice in Turnov from the beginning of the 17th century. Rudolph II, the Archduke of Austria, German Emperor and King of Hungary and Bohemia, was one of the first admirers of the stone, and he had a beautiful collection of uncut and worked garnets. In 1609, Boetius de Boot, the Emperor's doctor, confirmed that Rudolf indeed owned one of the largest garnet stones in the land.

## INTERNATIONAL FAME

The reputation of garnet spread outside the kingdom of Bohemia, and demand grew for it accordingly. In 1785, 187 jewellers were working with the stone in the Czech workshops. Seven years later, the total was 259.

became much more subtle and the metal component barely visible. The stone was so fashionable at the time that it became used in letter openers, photo frames, paper knives, powder compacts and cigarette cases. From 1900, jewellers began to work in the Art Nouveau style. Floral and ornamental motifs were incorporated into the design of brooches, combs and pendants, in which the garnets were set. This fashionable jewellery was exported all over the world and helped establish the international reputation of the Bohemian garnet.

There is a story that the ladies of the Russian court wore Turnov garnets in 1815 at the Vienna Congress to celebrate the defeat of Napoleon. The jewels travelled around the world and were seen at major exhibitions. There is a record of the unusual presence of Bohemian goldsmiths in Berlin in 1844, when they displayed their work there. Similarly, in Amsterdam in 1883, the Kratochvíl company won the silver medal for one of its pieces.

## GARNETS WITH EVERYTHING!

At the end of the 19th century, production diversified and garnets began to play a major part in the composition of the jewellery itself rather than simply as decoration. The settings

## GARNETS TODAY

Have a look in the jeweller's shop windows in Prague, and you'll find garnets of all shapes and sizes. On sale are rings, earrings, brooches, bracelets, pendants, lucky charms, hearts and crosses.

They tend to be rather classic in style but still retain a certain charm. A Czech garnet bought today could still remind you of your grandmother, since even contemporary pieces have a nostalgic feel about them. The balance between settings and stones has changed little since the end of the 19th century. The setting is often virtually hidden beneath all the small stones.

## GARNET CRAFTSMEN

The craftsmen's cooperative, known as Granát, is based in Turnov, garnet capital of Bohemia. It still makes traditional Czech jewellery today, and its current collection stands at 3,500 models. However, don't expect them to be very trendy. Most of the settings are in silver, silver-gilt or in 14/18 carat gold. You can try on pieces and purchase them from **Granát Turnov**, at Dlouhá 28-30, Staré Město (see p. 91).

## A LUCKY STONE

Mysterious powers have long been attributed to the garnet. Deep red in colour but at the same time almost transparent, it can look like a drop of blood, which is why it has been thought to have healing powers and to bring strength, energy, courage and even a happy temperament to those who wear it. As a symbol of blood, the garnet has been associated with the mystery of the Eucharist, and it often adorns liturgical pieces. The Strahov Monastery has good examples of this use, with its decorated gilded monstrances and crosses. The Klášter Premonstrátů na Strahově is at Strahovské nádvoří, Prague 1, and is open every day, 9am-12pm, 12.30-5pm.

# BEER – ELIXIR OF TRUTH AND LIFE

At 153 litres per capita per year, Czechs hold the world record for the consumption of beer. This isn't really surprising when you learn that the word *pivo*, which describes the national beverage, comes from the verb *piti*, meaning to drink, which is an activity that is central to Prague life. A 'Friends of Beer Party' was formed during the elections in 1990 and managed to recruit many thousands of members to its cause.

## CZECHS AND THEIR BEER

Beer has been consumed in Bohemia since the 11th century and reached the height of its popularity in the 13th century, thanks to King Václav I, who officially abolished the ban on brewing. It had carried the penalty of excommunication, although this was accorded very little respect. The unique quality of the beer is said to result from the perfect harmony between the barley used for making malt, the fine Bohemian hops and the extraordinarily soft local spring water. Since the 14th century, Bohemia has justifiably been acclaimed as the source of some of the best beers in the world.

## THE BIG TWO

Amongst the 400 brands of local beer, the most famous is the Plzeňský prazdroj ('original source'), better known by its German name Pilsner Urquell. The Bavarian

brewer, Josef Groll, first made the beer in 1842 in the town of Plzen (in German, Pilsen), situated 80km/50 miles from Prague. Its exceptional qualities explain why it has become a generic term, with Pils, Pilsner or Pilsener denoting a light beer with a distinctive hop flavour resulting from a second fermenting at low temperatures. Its only rival is none other than Budvar or Budweiser brewed in

České Budějovice (in German, Budweis), south of Prague. This is no relation to the American beer of the same name, although there are frequent hot disputes as to which of the brewing giants owns the copyright of the trademark.

## AND ONE VERY SPECIAL BEER...

U Fleků, at Kremencova, 11, is a classic beer hall where the house beer has been brewed since 1499 and is still sold there

today. It is a unique, strong and slightly sweet dark beer and large quantities are made each year and sold exclusively on these premises. Visit the beer garden in the summer and you will think you are at a tavern in Bavaria. One of the vaulted rooms has a cabaret at night.

## BEER YOU WON'T FIND ANYWHERE ELSE

There are three other famous local beers that you should try on your trip – Staropramen, Braník and Pražan. Taste the local brews,

Krušovice and Velkopopovický kozel. The latter is quite a strong beer and is easily recognisable by its label, showing a goat holding a glass of beer and no doubt the animal helps to add his own particular flavour to the brew!

## HOW TO DRINK BEER IN PRAGUE

Beer should be served at cellar temperature and with a head. To check its quality, see if a match can remain upright in the froth for ten seconds. After you have ordered and finished your first beer, your glass will be replaced automatically by the waiter, who marks a tab on the table. It is up to you to put a stop to the flow and to avoid becoming 'as drunk as a Dane', as the locals say.

## IT'S ALL IN THE PERCENTAGES

If you buy bottled beer, remember that the most obvious figure on the label (usually 10% or 12%) is not a reference to the alcohol content but rather to the density of malt used in the brew. The percentage of alcohol by volume is either in smaller type or not shown at all. As a general rule, divide the

density by three to work out the alcohol content. Beers can be bought in cans but these are principally for export. Local connoisseurs don't drink canned beer.

---

**BRIEF GLOSSARY OF TERMS FOR THE BEER DRINKER**

*Pivo:* beer
*Velké pivo:* large beer (50cl or just under a pint)
*Malé pivo:* small beer (30cl, larger than a half pint)
*Pivnice:* polite word for a pub or beer hall. Usual word is *hospoda* and *hostinec. Pivovar* is a generic term, meaning a pub.
*Pivní sýr:* soft and extremely pungent cheese mixed with chopped onions, paprika, then drowned in beer.
*Tekutý chléb:* local name for beer, meaning liquid bread.

# DANCES AND BALLS

Jan Neruda, poet and journalist, wrote widely about Prague. He captured the importance of dance, an essential part of Prague life and not just a pastime, when he said that 'the whole country sparkled like a ballroom dance floor and everyone danced on its musical soil'. The dance tradition began over a century ago, and is still immensely popular today. Every dance association makes it a point of honour to organise its own ball. Learning to dance when young is still considered a vital social skill.

### THOSE FIRST STEPS...

The Austrian aristocracy first held glamorous balls at the beginning of the 18th century in Prague's many palaces. A century later there were more than twenty dance halls in the city. People danced the Polonaise, the gavotte and the waltz, but soon the Czechs had mastered these and were ready to invent their own dances, such as the *Česká beseda* and the polka.

### DANCING FOR YOUR COUNTRY

The waltz took on a clearly political overtone through its strong links with the intense revival of the national movement at the beginning of the 19th century. From 1840, fervent patriots made their point with the organisation of the first 'Czech balls'. Thanks to the success of a major event organised in April 1848, the National Theatre was constructed with funds from private donations.

*Bedřich Smetana (1824-1884)*

Bedřich Smetana was an ardent nationalist, and dance became one of his favourite themes. In the greatest Czech opera, *The Bartered Bride*, Smetana takes popular polka tunes and reworks them, making a tribute at the end of the first act to this very energetic dance. Smetana was a German-speaker but was still the most nationalist of all Czech composers.

### LEARNING TO DANCE

Learning to dance the sacred polka and with it the waltz, tango, rumba and paso-doble, not to mention rock 'n' roll is an integral part of Prague education and boys and girls aged 15-17 are signed up for *Taneční* (dance classes).

The first ball offers them an opportunity to demonstrate their newly acquired talents to their mothers, in the glorious surroundings of Prague's ballrooms. The event marks their entry into society, and it is a highlight in the social calendar both for parents and pupils.

## POLKA

Make no mistake about the origins of the word polka – the Czechs are very sensitive about the matter. This jewel in the crown of national heritage did not come from Poland, as the name may suggest, but from Prague itself, at the start of the 19th century. The origin of the name of the dance is quite simple. The word *pul* means half, and the polka is a dance in double time. Many Czech composers have written scores for this swirling 'pas de deux' the most renowned being the *Škoda lásky* composed by Jaromír Vejvoda (1902-1988), which has become internationally famous under its American

*The popularity of the polka gradually spread throughout Europe as shown in this French print from the mid 19th century.*

name *Beer Barrel Polka*. Literally translated, it means 'love that has flown away'.

## THE SEASON

January to March marks the height of the ball season, but you'll find people enjoying a good dance all year round. Each profession has its own event, from firemen to chimney sweeps. There is even a Snobs' Ball. The grandest balls usually take place at the Lucerna Palace (see p. 55), the Žofín Palace (see p. 47) and at the Municipal House (see p. 61). The best way to fully appreciate their importance in Prague life is to take part in one of these evenings. Try to meet a few of the locals who might invite you. Failing this, just make your way to the Municipal House for a Saturday evening dance, between 6pm and midnight. Everyone is welcome to join in. Just put on your dancing shoes!

*Grand balls also take place at the Municipal House, where you can take part in a Czech tradition.*

## DANCE FEVER

It is usually in the month of February that the *maturitní ples* (graduation dance) takes place. It has become almost an initiation rite, with the nervous pupils obliged to ask the principal instructor to dance. The audience, made up of friends and family, show their support by raining money on the dancers, which is gathered up by the participants. They carry large nets to help them do this most effectively, proving that learning to dance has its rewards.

*The Žofín Palace hosts many balls.*

# FLAVOURS OF PRAGUE

Czech cooking has much in common with that of its Austrian and German neighbours. It is best described as 'Central European', with its robust winter fare, using lots of beef, pork, cabbage and fresh cream. The word 'light' does not spring to mind when describing it, but there are some specialities that are really delicious and which you really should try.

## TRADITIONAL FOOD

You'll soon discover that the same standard dishes appear on almost all restaurant menus. The national dish is pork served with dumplings and sauerkraut (*vepřové, knedlíky a zelí*). Equally popular is the dish known as *svíčková na smetaně*, which is a pot-roasted fillet of beef in a rich creamy sauce with a cranberry garnish. Hungarian *guláš* has found its second home here in Prague. You should enjoy this beef stew, with its very generous onion and paprika sauce.

## POLEVKA

A typical Prague meal starts with a simple soup known as *polévka*.

It can be potato soup (*bramboračka*), mushroom soup (*houbová*), or a beef and potato soup (*gulášová*). The true gourmet will enjoy chopped tripe soup (*dršťková*) sometimes generously spiced with paprika. A word of warning – always insist on your soup being served hot (*teplá*). There's a tendency for it to be brought to the table lukewarm.

## KNEDLIKY

Although dumplings are German in origin and name they play a very important

role in Bohemian cooking. They are a real speciality, but don't expect them to be like English dumplings. They resemble heavy white bread, and sliced dumplings accompany most hot dishes. They can be made with flour (*houskové*), grated potato and flour (*bramborové*) or bacon (*špekové*).

In Prague people don't spend much time over their meals. The locals tend to grab something to eat when they feel hungry and pop into a snack-bar (*bufet*) or a grocer's (*lahůdky*) to try one of their open sandwiches (*chlebíčky*). Follow their example and choose from a selection of ham, salami, gherkins, cream cheese, horseradish or salad with mayonnaise. Another option is to try the street stalls and have frankfurters (*párky*) or grilled sausages (*klobásy*) served with chunks of brown bread and mustard. Sausage stalls are very common in Central Europe and the locals either eat standing up or take the sausages away to eat cold. If you're hungry late in the evening, head for a *bufet*. They stay open late but not always all night.

Do give them a try, and if you are feeling very adventurous, you could also order fruit dumplings (*ovocné knedlíky*). These are served as a dessert with melted butter, icing sugar and poppy seeds.

## BREADCRUMBS
## WITH EVERYTHING!

*Smažený* is an important word in the Czech vocabulary. It means fried in breadcrumbs, and you will read it on every menu in every restaurant as it is the most common way of preparing food. You'll have a wide choice of breadcrumbed dishes, including cheese, escalopes, meatballs, cauliflower and carp.

These dishes can be excellent if fried well. Breaded and fried pork steak (*vepřový řízek*) is served with hot potatoes and a salad garnish with a slice of lemon. Try the *bramborák*, a potato pancake with salami and marjoram.

## PORK PRODUCTS

The famous Prague ham (*pražská šunka*) is often served as an appetiser with whipped cream and horseradish (*plněná šunka*). A slightly more sophisticated dish is made of pork sausage, sliced and marinated (or drowned) in vinegar (*utopenec*). You can buy salamis, sausages and other pork product in the many pork butchers in the city centre. The meat is delicious and low in fat, and it is particularly tasty when accompanied by gherkins. Make sure you try it at least once during your stay in Prague.

## CHRISTMAS CARP

Traditionally, the locals buy carp a week before Christmas. It is the main

dish eaten at the New Year's Eve celebrations. Street vendors set up their stalls in the city with barrels of fish, from which the locals make their selection. They're kept alive until 24 December, when they're then prepared in a variety of ways including carp soup, followed by fillets of carp fried in breadcrumbs and served with a potato salad. You'll find that winter salads are often pickled and in summer are composed of tomato, lettuce, cucumber and peppers with a simple dressing.

# Prague — practicalities

## GETTING AROUND THE CITY

If you're spending a weekend in Prague, it isn't necessary to have a car. You can explore Prague on foot or by public transport. Parking is prohibited for non-residents in the city centre, and spaces are at an absolute premium. You may find a wheel clamp (*botička*) attached to your car, in which case call the phone number on the document left on your windscreen or call the police. The fine will be at least Kč700. You are strongly advised to park in the monitored car parks, for example in Charles Square, where it will cost Kč10-30, or at one of the guarded car parks at the edge of the city or try the underground car parks on Národní Street, or by the main railway station.

If you arrive in the Czech Republic by car, you must buy an identification sticker at the border. The sticker is sold in petrol stations and post offices, and with it you are permitted to use the motorways (for a year). The speed limit on motorways is 130km per hr (81mph); in urban areas 60km per hr (37mph) and on dual and single carriageways 90km per hr (56mph).

If you drive, you must not drink any alcohol. Breath tests are frequent, even in the centre of the city and by law drivers are not permitted to have any alcohol in their blood.

## BY METRO AND TRAM

There are three lines on the underground. Line A is green and is the most useful for tourists. It covers all the main areas of the city centre and crosses from east to west. Line B is yellow and C is red. The service in the city and in the suburbs is quite frequent, daily 5am-midnight. Tickets (*jízdenky*) can be bought at the automatic ticket machines in the metro stations, in street kiosks, in tobacconists (*tabák*) or in hotels. Validate your ticket before taking the escalator into the underground. In the case of a tram, do this as you enter. Tickets are the same for both the metro and the tram, and a recorded message will announce each stop and the one to follow, together with the connections for the metro. Night trams operate from midnight until 5am, and they have two digit numbers, which always begin with 5.

Timetables and tram maps are available at every stop, and the trams are remarkably punctual. Take a 22 tram from the centre of Prague (Charles Square or Národní třída) to Prague Castle, crossing the Vltava and travelling via the Little Quarter (Malá Strana) – a lovely journey.

## THE FUNICULAR

Using your tram and train ticket, you can take the funicular railway up the wooded hill of Petřín and on to the station at Štefaníkova Hvězdárna, the Observatory.

From there the view is magnificent, and you can enjoy a lovely walk in the forest before returning to the city. Access to the funicular is at Újezd, 36, in the Malá Strana.

## HOW MUCH DOES IT COST?

The ticket costs Kč12 for up to 60 minutes travel time, with unlimited transfers, and Kč8 for 15 minutes without transfers. From 8pm-5am on weekdays and at weekends, the tickets are valid for 90 minutes. You must stamp your ticket in the little machine as soon as you board to validate it and be sure that you do, as random checks are carried out.

You can also buy a network ticket: Kč70 for 24 hours, Kč200 for three days, Kč250 for seven days and Kč280 for 15 days. These tickets, together with maps of the city, metro and tram systems, are all available from information centres and at automatic ticket machines in metro stations, including: **Muzeum station**, ☎ 22 64 01 03, Tue.- Sat., 7am-9pm, or the **Můstek station** beneath Jungmannovo Square, ☎ 22 64 63 50, Tue.-Sat., 7am-9pm. The staff speak English, German and French.

### BY BOAT

An alternative way to travel, which is quieter but more strenuous, is by small boat or pedalo. You can hire them on Slavic Island for one or two hours. Go to the front of the Žofín Palace on Masarykovo nábřeží.

After a long walk round the city, relax on a sunny day with a more leisurely journey aboard a boat along the Vltava river. An hour's trip costs around Kč150 and includes a drink. Choose from those on the Na Františku quay near the Čerchův most bridge. It is better to choose a small boat rather than a huge tourist-packed one. If you are looking for a longer journey outside Prague itself, then go to the pier on Rašínovo nábřeží, Prague 2 (metro station Charles Square, under the Palackeho most bridge). Conditions have to be right for this trip, and you may find that sometimes there's simply not enough water.

### CAR RENTAL

Having spent a weekend in Prague, you may feel tempted to explore outside the city. The most practical way is to hire a car. Take your driving licence and passport, and you can hire a Škoda Favorite or Felicia for about Kč700 per day. Contact one of the following:

**Vecar**
Svatovítská, 7
Prague 6
☎ 24 31 28 49
vecar@vecar.cz
Metro Dejvická.

**Hertz**
Karlovo náměstí, 28
Prague 1
☎ 22 23 10 10
www.hertz.com
Metro Karlovo.

**Rent a Car**
Washingtonova, 9
Prague 1
☎ 24 21 15 87
Metro Muzeum.

## MAKING A TELEPHONE CALL

There are many public phones in the city and in the metro stations. It's best to use phone card telephones rather than coin-operated ones, which are very rarely working. Buy a phone card from one of the news-stands (try Wenceslas Square), a tobacconist, a post office or a shop. You will pay Kč150 for 50 units, Kč240 for 80 units, Kč300 for 100 units, Kč360 for 120 units and Kč450 for 150 units.

For calls to the UK from Prague, dial 00 44; to Ireland dial 00 353; to Australia 00 61; to New Zealand 00 64; to the USA and Canada dial 00 1. For calls to Prague from the UK and Ireland dial 00 420 2; from the USA and Canada dial 011 420 2; and from Australia and New Zealand, dial 00 11 420 2.

If you have difficulty reaching a number in Prague, it could well have changed due to the current modernisation of the system. Call directory enquiries: ☎ 120 (numbers in Prague), ☎ 121 (outside Prague) and ask for an English-speaking operator, or try ☎ 0149 for international directory enquiries, which should have English speakers. Finally, ☎ 0132 is for help with international calls.

Within the Czech Republic itself, dial 02 to reach Prague. Within Prague dial the telephone number without the prefix 2.

Avoid making telephone calls from your hotel as you will incur a heavy surcharge. The dialling code is a short note and then a long one. Long regular notes indicate the ringing tone wheras the engaged signal is a series of short rapid notes.

## POSTING A LETTER

You can buy stamps (*poštovní známka*) with your postcards or at the post office. Post boxes are easily recognisable and are bright orange. The Main Post Office (*Hlavní pošta*) is at Jindřišská, 14,

Prague 1, close to Wenceslas Square, ☎ 113 11 11. It's pretty large, so you shouldn't miss it, and is open 24 hours a day, with a reduced service at night. You can send and receive faxes from here on ☎ (00 42 02) 23 20 837. There's another post office in the Old Town, near metro Staroměstská on Kaprova 12, Prague 1. To send a postcard within Europe costs 9Kč (15Kč for a letter). Elsewhere it is 7Kč (11Kč for a letter.)

## CHANGING MONEY

Don't even contemplate exchanging money on the black market on the streets of Prague – you will almost certainly be conned, and many of these crooks have serious-looking minders. Use the banks or the bureaux de change, which stay open fairly late (although watch the rates in the exchange booths in touristy areas – they really hike the rates if you change small amounts). You can also withdraw cash at ATM machines, which accept debit and all major credit cards.

**American Express**
Wenceslas Square, 56
☎ 22 80 02 11
open Mon.-Fri. 9am-6pm,
Sat. 9am-noon.

**Komerční banka**
Na příkope, 33
☎ 22 43 21 11
Open Mon.-Fri. 8-11am, 1-6pm.

**Obchodní banka**
Na příkope, 14
Open Mon.-Fri., 7.30am-
noon, 1-3.30pm.

**Živnostenská banka**
Na příkope, 20
☎ 24 12 11 11
Open Mon.-Fri. 8am-9pm,
Sat. 1pm-5pm.

The 24 hour exchange desk
at the airport is run by the
Československá Obchodni
Bank.

# TOURIST INFORMATION OFFICES

**Pražská Informační
Služba (P.I.S.)**
Na příkope, 24
☎ 26 40 20
Open Mon.-Fri. 9am-6pm,
Sat.-Sun. 9am-3pm.
With its easily identifiable
three-pronged crown logo,
you'll find the P.I.S.
a valuable and reliable
source for detailed
information and maps
as well as various
programmes of cultural
events. They also have
a website which is
worth checking out
before you even
leave home:
www.prague-info.cz

**Čedok**
Na příkope, 18
☎ 24 19 73 19

Open Mon.-Fri. 9am-7pm,
Sat. 10am-3pm.
This is a useful place for
general information, train
and bus timetables and
international tickets. Some
credit cards are accepted.

For tourist information by
phone, in English or German,
call ☎ 54 44 44/45/46/47.

# OPENING HOURS

Museums and galleries are
generally open from 9-10am
until 5-6pm every day except
Monday. Churches operate
similar hours, and some charge
an entry fee. You may find
you're unable to enter some
churches as they're undergoing
reconstruction. In the Jewish
quarter, the synagogues and
shops are closed on Saturdays.

## EMBASSIES

**British Embassy**
Thunovská 14, Prague 1
☎ 57 53 02 78
www.britain.cz

**Irish Embassy**
Tržiště 13, Prague 1
☎ 57 53 00 61

**American Embassy**
Tržiště 15, Prague 1
☎ 57 32 06 63

**Canadian Embassy**
Mickiewiczova 6, Prague 1
☎ 72 10 18 00

**Australian Honorary Consul**
Na Ořechovce 38, Prague 6
☎ 24 31 07 43

**New Zealand Honorary
Consul**
☎ 25 41 98
(for emergency use only).

Tourists have to pay an entry
charge of Kč400 for the
cemetery and synagogue only,
but students will get a
reduction on presentation of
their student ID card (see p. 9).

# TOILETS AND REST ROOMS

They are usually
marked 'WC', which is
pronounced 'vay-tsay'
and there is often a
charge of around
Kč10, in return for
which you may also
be handed a few
sheets of toilet paper.
The word for Mens is
*Páni* or *Muži* and for
Ladies is *Dámy* or *Ženy*.
You can usually find a number
of public toilets about and
there are toilets in every
metro station.

# Hradčany

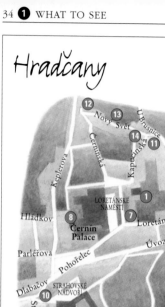

The third of Prague's five towns, Hradčany was founded around 1320. A terrible fire destroyed the medieval district in 1541, so much of the area was then rebuilt, but little has changed since and Hradčany stands looking down over the city and river much as it did centuries ago.

## ❶ The Loreto (Loreta)★★★

Loretánské nám., 7
Open Tue.-Sun. 9am-12.15pm, 1pm-4.30pm
Entry charge.

Kryštof Dientzenhofer was responsible for the stunning Baroque façade of this place of pilgrimage. Within the complex is a copy of what is thought to be the Virgin Mary's house. On the first floor of the cloister is the magnificent Treasury, in which you will see a gold-plated monstrance, piously bequeathed in 1699 by Countess Ludmilar de Kolovrat and encrusted with a mere 6,222 diamonds.

## ❷ Šternberg Palace (Šternberský Palác)★★

Hradčanské nám., 15
☎ 20 51 46 34
Open Tue.-Sun. 10am-6pm
Entry charge.

Count Šternberg donated this Baroque palace to the Society

of Patriotic Friends of the Arts in Bohemia, which he founded in 1796. The palace houses a selection of works from the Italian, Flemish and German schools of the 15th to 18th centuries. Don't miss *The Feast of the Rosary* by Dürer (1506). Emperor Rudolph II ordered that the painting be brought from Venice on a man's back.

## ❸ Schwarzenberg Palace (Schwarzenberský Palác)★

Hradčanské nám., 2
Open Tue.-Sun. 10am-6pm.

The palace houses a permanent exhibition called Monuments

of the Nation's Past, which includes documents, paintings, jewellery, sculpture and weapons. The complex of buildings dates from 1570, and some of the original sgraffito on the façade can still be seen.

## ❹ U Zavěšenýho Kafe★

Radnické Schody
Open every day 11am-midnight.

In his tiny café, Jakub Krejí is able to display his works on the wall and serve large beers

to customers sitting on long wooden tables. It's like a mountain chalet inside. If you are feeling brave, try the *pivní sýr* (cheese with beer) or the *nakládaný hermelín* (marinated camembert). These are house specialities with very powerful flavours.

## ❺ Navavila Design★

Radnické Schody, 9
☎ 20 51 38 68
Open every day
10am-6pm.

Martina Nevařilová provides a welcoming and friendly oasis for those looking for stylish clothes in what is a near desert for fashion. You'll find jumpers and woollen

dresses with exotic touches from Central Europe. Choose an interesting hat or unusual gloves from a big selection of originals.

## ❻ Hradčany Square (Hradčanské náměstí)★★

This square commands the most prestigious position, much prized by Czech nobility. The Lobkowicz, Schwarzenberg, Thun-Hohenstein, Martinic and

Sternberg families competed to outdo each other in this location, as the various places bearing their names testify. Alfons Mucha (see p. 14) lived in the Baroque house at no. 6, where part of Forman's film *Amadeus* was set.

### ❼ U Loivety★★

Loretánské nám., 8
☎ 20 51 73 69
Open every day 11am-11pm.

This restaurant has a terrace overlooking the Loreto and Hradčany. Try their duck with cabbage and dumplings, and enjoy a glass of Moravian wine. Despite its strategic position, this old-style restaurant, with its great Czech cuisine classics, has not yet succcumbed to the compulsory face-lift underway elsewhere. It would be a shame to miss it.

### ❽ ČERNIN PALACE (ČERNINSKÝ PALÁC)★★

Loretánské nám.
Closed to public.

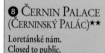

Having quarrelled with Bernini, Count Cernin commissioned Francesco Caratti to complete the 150m/500ft façade, decorated with thirty Palladian half-columns. It was finally finished three centuries later (1669-1936). Just days after the Communist coup in 1948, Jan Masaryk, popular son of Czechoslovakia's first President, Tomáš Masaryk, fell to his death from one of the windows of the Ministry of Foreign Affairs.

### ❾ Peklo (Hell)★

Strahovské nádvoří
☎ 20 51 00 32
Open every day 6pm-2am.

Despite its rather alarming name, you can enter without fear into this restaurant in the old cellars of Strahov Monastery. There's a choice of Czech or Italian food but its location is more impressive than its menu. No doubt it was the monks who were responsible for naming this place of temptation.

### ❿ The Strahov Monastery★★★

Strahovské nádvoří, 1
Open every day 9am-5pm
Entry charge.

The monastery was founded in 1140 by a French religious order, the Premonstratensians, and they remained here, except for an enforced eviction during the Communist period. Make a point of visiting the impressive libraries. Look around the Theological Hall (1679) with its extensive stucco and its wall paintings, and visit the Philosophical Hall (1782), named in tribute to the Age of Enlightenment.

### ⓫ U Zlaté Hrušky (The Golden Pear)★★

Nový Svět, 3
☎ 20 51 47 78
Open every day 11.30am-3pm, 6.30pm-midnight.

Dishes such as venison in red wine and duck with honey and almonds are on the menu at this restaurant which specialises in game, situated in a 16th-century house. You can eat in the garden in summer, and you'll enjoy excellent Czech dishes. Haunt of the rich and famous (Mick Jagger, Meryl Streep and Tom Cruise have all dined here), and this is reflected in the prices. The cuisine by a Czech chef is exquisite. Reservations essential.

## **12** Pension U Raka★★

Černínská, 10
☎ 20 51 11 00
🖷 20 51 05 11

Here's a bit of countryside in the heart of the city. This half-timbered cottage dates from the end of the 18th century and has six lovely rooms. It's the perfect hideaway, which does not allow children or dogs. You can just enjoy a cup of tea or a glass of Moravian wine, if the accommodation is beyond your budget. Ring the bell

and you'll be greeted by a cheerful host.

## **13** New World (Nový Svět)★

Here you'll see a totally different scale of living from that of Hradčany Square. To make it clear that they were not ashamed of their poverty, the

### **14** NOVÝ SVĚT GALLERY★★

Nový Svět, 5
☎ 20 51 46 11
Open every day 10am-6pm.

Jana Reichová opened this renovated and dynamic gallery in 1994, celebrating the 300th anniversary of the Baroque building in which it's housed. In the basement (originally the coal cellar), there are regular exhibitions of the works of the best contemporary artists. On the ground floor, under a fresco of St John Nepomuk, patron of Hradčany and canonised in 1729, you'll discover the photographs of Josef Sudek, glass pieces by Šípek and drawings and engravings by Theimer, Sopko or Sládek. There are beautiful art books and carefully selected copies of antique glasses, costing from just Kč100 up to as much as Kč200,000.

14th-century castle workers gave their humble cottages golden house signs. You'll spot a golden pear, a grape, a bush and an acorn. The houses are now being renovated, and no doubt prices in this peaceful and charming area will soon escalate.

# Josefov and the Jewish ghetto

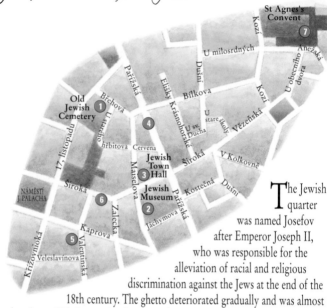

The Jewish quarter was named Josefov after Emperor Joseph II, who was responsible for the alleviation of racial and religious discrimination against the Jews at the end of the 18th century. The ghetto deteriorated gradually and was almost reduced to rubble in 1893 by the city authorities, so that now only a few winding lanes remain. The Golem, Prague's notorious monster, supposedly given life by Rabbi Löw in th 16th century, is said to wander these streets at night, so keep an eye out for him.

## ❶ Old Jewish Cemetery★★★

U starého hřbitova, 3
☎ 23 17 191 or 23 10 302
Open every day except
Sat. 9am-5pm (Nov.-Mar.
9am-4.30pm)
Entry charge includes Jewish
Museum.

There are over 12,000 gravestones in this very tiny space, and it is estimated that 100,000 people are buried here. The oldest grave dates back to 1439 and the most recent to 1787. It certainly is a remarkable site. Rabbi Löw's

tombstone is the most visited, and pebbles and little notes are frequently left upon it.

## ❷ Jewish Museum★★

Jáchymova, 3
☎ 24 81 00 99
Open every day except
Sat. 9am-6pm (Nov.-Mar.
9am-4.30pm)
Entry charge.

Of the six Prague synagogues, only the Old-New Synagogue (1270) is still in active use. Some of the others house different sections of the Jewish Museum, whose exceptional diversity and richness is said to have come about, paradoxically, from the Nazis' own intention to create a museum for the people they planned to eliminate. On the walls of the Pinkas Synagogue are the names of 77,297 Czech victims of the Nazis. In the former ceremonial hall hang the paintings of children deported to Terezín concentration camp.

### ❸ Jewish Town Hall★

Maiselova, 18
☎ 24 81 11 21
Closed to the public.

The Jewish Town Hall was built between 1570 and 1577, and one of its clocks has Hebrew figures and hands that turn in an anti-clockwise direction (just as Hebrew reads from right to left). Visit the Shalom restaurant (open every day except Sat. 11.30am-2pm), which serves kosher food.

### ❹ Pařížská★★

This vast avenue with its elegant neo-Baroque, neo-Gothic and Secession façades was based on Haussman's Parisian model, hence its name. International airline

offices and boutiques fill the ground floor premises. The road runs through the heart of Josefov.

### ❺ Alma★

Valentinská, 7
☎ 23 25 865
Open every day 10am-6pm.

Both café and antique shop,

Alma has a lovely nostalgic feel. Goulash is served as a house speciality, but do try a strudel and a cup tea if you are not in the mood for a spicy dish. After a delicious meal, you can buy that Art Nouveau lamp or piece of Art Deco jewellery of your dreams, but don't expect a bargain.

### ❼ St Agnes's Convent★

U milosrdných, 17
☎ 24 81 06 28
Open every day 10am-6pm.

This convent was founded in 1234 by Agnes, sister of King Wenceslas I. It became one of Bohemia's principal religious centres, and, by a startling coincidence, St Agnes was

### ❻ CAFÉ COLONIAL*

Široká, 6
☎ 24 81 83 22
Open Mon-Sat. 10am-midnight, Sun. 8.30am-5pm.

If you are suffering from an overdose of sausages and cabbage, pop into this café for some culinary relief. It's run by Marie Borenstein, from Belgium, and Marlene Salomon, from France. They opened the café in 1997 and serve crisp salads and tasty concoctions. The light and bright interior offers a welcome change from the smoky taverns. It's a favourite haunt of French expatriates and artists.

canonised only a few weeks before the November 1989 revolution. You'll find Czech paintings and sculptures from the 19th century, belonging to the National Gallery. These are comparatively unknown but well worth discovering.

# Karlovo náměstí (Charles square)

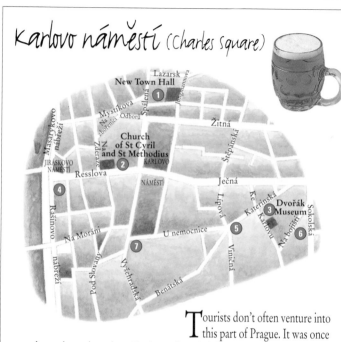

New Town Hall ①
Lazarsk
New Town Hall
Mystíkova
Na
Odboru
Zítná
Church
of St Cyril
and St Methodius ②
KARLOVO
JIRÁSKOVO
NÁMĚSTÍ
Resslova
NÁMĚSTÍ
Ječná
④
Dvořák
Museum ③
Rašínovo
Na Moráni
⑤
⑥
U nemocnice
⑦
Pod Slovany
Vyšehradská
Benátská

Tourists don't often venture into this part of Prague. It was once the cattle market when Charles IV founded the New Town in 1348. Now the main commercial district, those living near the river walk their dogs in the square, trams cross its main streets and everything seems calm and peaceful. However, do not be deceived. It was here that Faust dabbled in black magic and made a pact with the devil.

## ❶ New Town Hall★

Karlovo nám., 23
Closed to the public.

On the largest square in Prague stands this fine Gothic hall, which houses prestigious exhibitions and can be hired for lavish wedding receptions. It was here that the first 'defenestration' in Prague took place. During a Hussite revolt on 30 July 1419, the burghers were thrown out of the windows and landed on the pikes of the Hussites. A statue of Hussite preacher Jan Želivský commemorates this.

## ❷ Church of St Cyril and St Methodius★

Resslova, 9
Open Mon.-Sat.
9-11am

This Baroque church, built in the

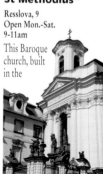

1730s, became the base for the Czechoslovak Orthodox Church in 1935 and was rededicated to the two saints. These brothers, known as 'Apostles to the Slavs' brought Christianity to Moravia in the 9th century. In 1942, the parachutists who had assassinated the Nazi governor of Czechoslovakia, Reinhard Heydrich, hid in the church, and you can still see the bullet holes left in the crypt by the machine guns used against them. They took their own lives rather than surrender.

The Canadian-born Frank Gehry and the Yugoslav-born Vlado Milunic designed this glass building. It looks rather like a couple dancing, hence its nickname. The fashionable French restaurant, La Perle de Prague, is housed here. Before moving to a more discreet home, Václav Havel lived next door.

## **3** Dvořák Museum★★

Ke Karlovu, 20
Open Tue.-Sun. 10am-5pm.

The museum not only houses Dvořák's piano, desk and viola, but also has some more unusual memorabilia, such as a handkerchief, cuffs, a hat and a medicine case. This lovely Baroque villa, dating from the 18th century is hidden at the bottom of a garden. Formerly the second home of a rich Bohemian family, it became known as Villa Amerika after a nearby inn. It was a perfect name for the composer of the *New World Symphony*.

## **4** Fred and Ginger★★

Rašínovo nábř., 80
☎ 21 98 41 60
Open Mon. 7pm-10.30pm, Tue.-Sat. noon-2pm and 7pm-10.30pm.

## **5** St Catherine Bazaar★

Kateřinská, 14
☎ 24 91 01 23
Open Mon.-Fri. 10am-6pm.

This is not just a bric-à-brac market. It's a journey through time. Jiří Pechar has lovingly collected stuffed birds, assorted plates and glasses,

wooden mannequins, tools and kitchen utensils in this unlikely venue. You can rummage around and bargain to your heart's content. You might find just what you've been looking for but the prices aren't cheap.

## **7** Faust House★

Karlovo nám., 40-41
Closed to the public.

A mysterious aura surrounds this Baroque house, where it's claimed that the devil abducted Faust. The English adventurer and alchemist, Edward Kelley, came to live here but was later thrown in prison by Emperor Rudolph II. He failed to reveal the secret of the philosopher's stone to the Emperor, a keen follower of necromancy. Appropriately enough, there is now a pharmacy on the ground floor of the building.

## **6** U Kalicha★

Na Bojišti, 12-14
☎ 29 19 45
Open every day 11am-10pm.

The atmosphere in this pub has much in common with a Munich *Oktoberfest* with beer served in large jugs. It's based on the theme of the famous Czech comic character, the good soldier Švejk. Jaroslav Hašek's hero walks in and suddenly finds himself arrested in connection with the assassination of Archduke Ferdinand. Traditional Czech cuisine is served, but tourists rather than locals come to eat here.

# Prague Castle, a town within a town

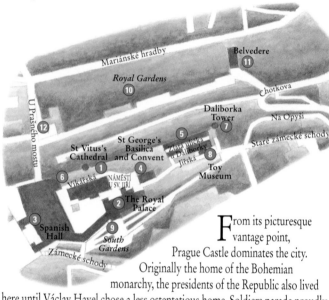

Mariánské hradby

Royal Gardens
**10**

Belvedere
**11**

Chotkova

U Prašného mostu

**12**

Daliborka
Tower
**7**

Na Opyši

Staré zámecké schody

St Vitus's
Cathedral
**1**

St George's
Basilica
and Convent
**4**

**5**
Zlatá ulička
u Daliborky
Jiřská

**8**

Toy
Museum

Vikářská

NÁMĚSTÍ
U SV. JIŘÍ

**6**

**2** The Royal
Palace

**3** Spanish
Hall

**9**
South
Gardens

Zámecké schody

From its picturesque
vantage point,
Prague Castle dominates the city.
Originally the home of the Bohemian
monarchy, the presidents of the Republic also lived
here until Václav Havel chose a less ostentatious home. Soldiers parade proudly
at noon everyday to the sound of trumpets. Take a close look at their uniforms
with their gold buttons. They were designed by Teodor Pištěk, costume
designer to Miloš Forman, the film director. For those of you just wanting
to relax, there are several cafés and restaurants within the castle precincts.

### ❶ St Vitus's Cathedral★★★
Second courtyard.

The French architect Matthew
of Arras began work on the
mighty Gothic cathedral in
1344, but it was not completed
until 1929. The Rococo tomb
of St John Nepomuk was
crafted from two tons of solid
silver in 1736. The magnificent
Art Nouveau stained glass
window by Alfons Mucha
features St Cyril and
St Methodius. Be sure to
visit St Wenceslas Chapel,

where the walls are decorated
with polished semi-precious
stones from Bohemia.

## ❷ The Royal Palace★★★

Third Courtyard.

Fortified in the 11th century, the oldest part of the Castle was inhabited by Czech kings until the Habsburgs established their residency in Vienna in the 17th century. The massive Gothic Vladislav Hall, with its magnificent rib vaulting, was designed by Benedikt Ried in the 1490s and is enormous and breathtaking. The former tournament hall, in which knights gathered on horseback for indoor jousting competitions, is now the place where Václav Havel was sworn into office as President of the Republic in 1989. The hall dominates the whole of the palace structure, which has three distinct levels constructed at different times. The impressive palace was extensively restored in 1924.

## ❸ Spanish Hall★★

Second Courtyard
Closed to the public.

The Central Committee of the Communist Party met for many years beneath the gilded chandeliers of this hall before it became a reception room for prestigious events. Sadly, it is out of bounds to the public, but concerts are occasionally held in this stunning room.

## ❹ St George's Basilica and Convent★★

Jiřské nám., 33

Hidden behind the Baroque façade is the best preserved Romanesque basilica in Prague, rebuilt after a fire in 1142. The first rulers of Bohemia, the Premyslids, rest here, and the Convent of the same name houses a very extensive and magnificent collection of Czech art of the Gothic, Renaissance and Baroque periods, including 14th century portraits by Master Theodoric and Baroque works by Karel Škréta, Peter Brandl and Matyáš Braun.

*The colourful cottages in the castle's Golden Lane (see p. 44)*

The convent was Bohemia's first monastery, founded in 973 by Prince Boleslav II, whose sister Mlada was its first abbess.

### ROCK N' ROLL

Bizarrely enough, the magnificent Spanish Hall built in the 17th century has good reason to thank a very unlikely and modern benefactor in the form of one of the West's longest-lived and best-known rock groups. During their 1995 tour The Rolling Stones brought their considerable entourage to Prague and played to a huge crowd of more than 100,000 people. Afterwards the group donated a large sum of money to the city to pay for the installation of a new lighting system in the Spanish Hall. As a result of their generous donation, its beams, chandeliers and trompe l'oeil murals are now illuminated to great effect. It's indeed a pity that few of the general public are able to see it for themselves.

### ❺ Golden Lane★★★

(Zlatá Ulička)

It's claimed that Emperor Rudolph II housed his alchemists in the tiny multi-coloured cottages, which were built into the walls of the Gothic fortifications. The shops in these tiny premises make their own pots of gold today by selling locally-made crafts and souvenirs of all kinds. Kafka lived in no. 22 from 1917-18, and he remains one of the street's most famous inhabitants.

### ❻ Vikárka★

Vikářská, 6
☎ 57 32 06 04

This tavern has been within the walls of Prague Castle since the 15th century. You can feast on a Charles IV tournedos steak and other dishes with royal and impressive names. You might even be lucky enough to encounter Václav Havel himself. He likes to drop in during his lunchbreak from time to time.

### ❼ Daliborka Tower★

The tower was used as a prison until 1781 and bears the name of its first inmate, Dalibor of Kozojedy, later immortalised in Smetana's opera. The citizens of Prague demanded his release, moved by his skill as a violinist. However, the prisoner did not manage to escape his fate and was beheaded in 1498.

### ❽ Toy Museum★★

Jiřská, 6
☎ 33 37 22 94
Open every day 9.30am-5.30pm

Having created the Munich Toy Museum, Ivan Šteiger returned from exile in Germany to build a museum for Prague, telling the story of toys for the past 150 years. In its seven magical rooms you will find miniature trains, tin toys, old stuffed bears, dolls' house furniture and hundreds of Barbie dolls.

### ❾ South Gardens (Jižní zahrady)★

Prague Castle (access from Hradčany Square)
Open every day Apr.-Oct.
10am-6pm
Entry free.

As a gesture of democracy, President Havel reopened these charming small gardens in 1990. They are situated on the ramparts of the Castle and have an uninterrupted view over the Old Royal Palace and the rooftops of the Little Quarter. There are two obelisks, which mark the spot where two governors, thrown from a window, landed safely during the defenestration of 1618. This marked the prelude to the Thirty Years War.

### ❿ Royal Garden (Královská zahrada)★★

Prague Castle,
U Prasneho mostu
Open every day Apr.-Oct.
10am-6pm
Entry free.

Not to be confused with the South Gardens, the Royal Garden was designed according to Renaissance principles

The Castle grounds open every day 5am-midnight (6am-11pm Nov.-Mar.). The buildings open every day 9am-5pm (9am-4pm Nov.-Mar.). You can buy a range of tickets, the cheapest option allowing you into four of the attractions open to the public. These are available in any of the buildings or at the information centre in the chapel of St Kříž, in the second courtyard. ☎ 24 37 33 68 or 24 31 08 96

for Ferdinand I in 1535. The tulips that bloom in the spring are a distant echo of those the Emperor had brought back

from Turkey by his ambassadors. He was the first to grow the flowers in Europe, despite the harsh winters in Bohemia.

### ⓫ Belvedere (Belvedér)★★

Prague Castle, Royal Garden

Ferdinand I built this lovely summer house for his beloved wife Anne. You can just picture the receptions and balls given in her honour. It's a fine Italian Renaissance building, built by Paolo della Stella and completed in 1564. Don't miss the Singing Fountain (1568), which owes its name to the musical sound the water makes as it hits the bronze bowl.

### ⓬ Arcimboldo Restaurant ★

U Prašného mostu, 6
☎ 24 31 01 71
Open every day noon-midnight.

Situated at the northern entrance to the Castle, this restaurant was recently renovated. It bears the name of Guiseppe Arcimboldo, who painted fruit and vegetables for Emperor Rudolph II. There's a wide range of game dishes, inspired by 17th-century recipes. For a simpler and quicker meal opt for the adjoining Café Cattedrala.

Rudolfinum
J. PALACHA NÁMĚSTÍ
Kaprova
Museum of Decorative Arts
KARLŮV MOST
KŘIŽOVNICKÉ NÁMĚSTÍ
Karlova
Smetana Museum
Smetanovo nábřeží
Karoliny Světlé
Divadelní
Národní
MOST LEGIÍ
Gastro Žofín
Slovanský ostrov
Masarykovo nábřeží
Mánes Art Gallery

# Beneath Charles Bridge runs the Vltava River

A ll roads lead to Charles Bridge, Prague's most familiar monument and home to craft and souvenir stalls galore. A steady stream of tourists strolls across the medieval bridge, buying trinkets. Its fame is due mostly to the 30 magnificent Baroque statues which line each side, though when first built its only decoration was a simple bronze crucifix. The river Vltava running beneath provides relief to the landlocked Czechs when they tire of city life and go in search of broader vistas.

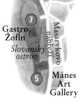

## ❶ Charles Bridge (Karlův most)★★★

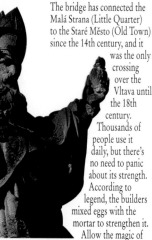

The bridge has connected the Malá Strana (Little Quarter) to the Staré Město (Old Town) since the 14th century, and it was the only crossing over the Vltava until the 18th century. Thousands of people use it daily, but there's no need to panic about its strength. According to legend, the builders mixed eggs with the mortar to strengthen it. Allow the magic of this spot to do its work, and run the gauntlet of the thirty statues at dawn or at dusk. It's an unforgettable experience.

## ❷ Rudolfinum★

Nám. Jana Palacha, 1
☎ 24 89 32 05.

This splendid example of neo-Renaissance architecture bears the name of the Austrian archduke, Rudolph of Habsburg. It is now the home of the Czech Philharmonic Orchestra. Some of the most impressive concerts in the Prague Spring music festival have been held in the sumptuous Dvořák Hall.

### ❸ Museum of Decorative Arts (Uměleckoprůmyslové Muzeum)★

17 Listopadu, 2
☎ 51 09 31 11
Open
Tue.-Sun.
10am-6pm
Entry
charge.

The museum
has a unique
collection of
furniture, rugs, clocks
and glass, which range
in style from Renaissance
to Biedermeier.
The very best
of Bohemian art
is on display in
one of the most
fascinating museums
in the city. There's an
excellent café, which is
the favourite haunt of students
of the decorative arts.

### ❹ Smetana Museum (Museum Bedřicha Smetany)★

Novotného lávka, 1
☎ 24 22 90 75
Open every day exc. Tue. 10am-5pm.

A former neo-
Renaissance
waterworks
has been
converted
into a
memorial
to Bedřich
Smetana, and
the museum
stands on a spit of land
beside the river.
This is an ideal
location for
the composer
of *Vltava*, part

of the cycle of symphonic
poems known as *Ma Vlast*
(*My Fatherland*). The museum
contains his piano together
with scores, documents and
letters detailing the life of the
most nationalist of great Czech
composers.

### ❺ Mánes Art Gallery★

Masarykovo
nábřeží, 1
Open every day exc.
Sun. 10am-6pm.

This white functionalist
building was
completed in 1932
and is named
after Josef Mánes,
a 19th-century
landscape painter. The
gallery has interesting
exhibitions and a café
with a stunning river
view.

### ❻ Národní Banka vín★★

Platnéřská, 4
☎ 21 10 82 44
Open Mon.-Fri.
10am-7pm,
Sat.-Sun. 1-6pm.

### ❼ Gastro Žofín★

Žofín, 226
☎ 90 00 06 63
Open every day 11am-midnight.

This huge yellow building
dominates the island
known as Žofín, named
after Sophie, mother of
Emperor Franz-Josef I.
The island was the result
of natural silting of the river
in the 18th century. Lavish
balls were held in the
building at the end of the
19th century by the cream
of Prague society, and
concerts still take place
today. In summer you can
enjoy sitting on the terrace
of this restaurant, which
serves robust Czech food.
If you're feeling romantic,
hire a boat and row with
your loved one down the
river. Boats are available for
hire from May-October.

In the cellars of St Francis's
Church is a 'wine bank' for
storing maturing wines, that
has been blessed by the papal
nuncio to the Czech Republic.
Here you can select a good
Moravian wine, with the
benefit of Adéla Andráková's
advice and knowledge, gained
through her studies in France.

# Malá Strana,
## the aristocratic Little Quarter

Malá Strana, or the Little Quarter, was founded in the 13th century on the slopes below the Castle. It reached the height of its splendour when the Catholic nobility built their sumptuous palaces there after the Battle of the White Mountain in 1620. You'll see many fine buildings, some of which are now foreign embassies. The area has retained much of its traditional character. To enjoy the romantic and mysterious atmosphere, wander along the narrow cobbled streets and then relax in one of the many cafés on Nerudova street. You'll be spoilt for choice.

### ❶ Little Quarter Square (Malostranské náměstí)★★

The houses around the square (founded in 1257) were originally built in the Middle Ages but rebuilt in the Renaissance and the Baroque periods. The square divides around the Church of St Nicholas and in its centre is a column which marks the end of a plague epidemic in 1713.

### ❷ Church of St Nicholas★★★

Malostranské nám.
☎ 232 25 89
Open every day 9am-5pm
Entry charge.

This church, a family masterpiece, is the most magnificent Jesuit-influenced Baroque building in the city. Krystof Dientzenhofer began work on it in 1703, followed by his son Kilian Ignaz, and Kilian's son-in-law, Anselmo Lugaro, completed the building in 1755. You'll get the best view of the statues, frescoes and paintings by going to one of the concerts. Mozart himself played the organ in the Church in 1787.

### ❸ Church of St Thomas★★

Letenská, 12
☎ 530 218
Open only for services,
Mon. & Wed. 6pm, Sun. 10am,
11.30am & 6pm.

Kilian Ignaz Dientzenhofer was also responsible for this church, but this time on his own. It was built to replace a Gothic church destroyed in the Hussite wars. The two Rubens above the altar are copies.

The originals are in the National Gallery, now housed in Prague's Sternberg Palace (see p. 34).

## ❹ St Thomas's Brewery★

Near the church
☎ 530 218
Open every day 11.30am–11pm.

The Augustinian monks first brewed beer at St Thomas's in 1352. It was such

a tasty brew that they became sole purveyor to Prague Castle. There are three beer halls in the basement, where you can now enjoy a dark beer from the Braník brewery.

## ❺ Nerudova Street★★

This street is named after the 19th century writer Jan Neruda, author of many short stories set in this part of Prague. He lived in the houses called The Two Suns (no. 47) and The Three Black Eagles (no. 44). Look out for the Morzin Palace (no. 5, the Rumanian Embassy), which has two massive statues of moors (a pun on the owner's name). These were the work of the sculptor Ferdinand Maximilián Brokof. The Thun-Hohenstein Palace (no. 20, now the Italian embassy) is a grand Baroque building.

rooftops of Prague. You can see into the hidden courtyards of the Little Quarter and behind its secret façades. The garden was designed in the 18th century and has a lovely pavilion. Three gardens belonging to the former Ledebour, Černin and Pálffy palaces are linked together, and they have recently been restored. Enjoy the Tuscan-style balustraded terraces in this maze of a garden, and wander through the Classical statues, old fountains and ornamental urns. Choose a pleasant spot by the vines and water plants to enjoy the superb view.

## ❻ Ledebour Garden (Ledeburská zahrada)★★

Valdštejnská 3
Open every day 10am–7pm
Entry charge.

From the steps to the garden you'll be treated to a spectacular view of the

### **7 Wallenstein Palace and Garden**★★

Valdštejnské nám., 4
Riding School open every day
exc. Mon. 9am-6pm
Garden open every day
May-Sept. 9am-7pm

This early Baroque palace was built in 1624-30 for Count Albrecht of Wallenstein. Over thirty houses, three churches and the municipal brick kiln were destroyed to make way for the building. Emperor Ferdinand II appointed Wallenstein as imperial military commander, and the latter had a portrait painted of himself as Mars on the ceiling of a palace room now used for state functions. The former riding school currently houses exhibitions by the National Gallery. There are copies of works by Adriaen de Vries, the originals having been stolen by the invading Swedes in 1648.

### **8 Pálffy Palace**★★

Valdštejnská, 14
☎ 57 32 05 70
Open every day 11am-3pm,
6-11pm.

This Baroque palace is home to the conservatoire of music and a restaurant with a wonderful atmosphere. Dine by candle-light in beautiful surroundings

with the most fashionable locals. The food is an unusual combination of Czech and Californian culinary styles.

### **9 Maltese Square (Maltézské nám.)**★★

Grand palaces surround this square, and several embassies seem to be competing for the prize of the most elegant. Cast your own vote after looking at the flamboyant Baroque Nostitz Palace (no. 1), which houses the Dutch embassy, and the more austere Order of Malta (no. 4). Or you may find yourself swayed instead by the pink Rococo Turba Palace (no. 6), home to the Japanese embassy.

### **10 Buquoy Palace**★★

Velkopřevorské nám.
Closed to the public.

The French embassy is located in a delightful

Baroque building (1738), in which Miloš Forman filmed several of the scenes for his film *Amadeus*, which features numerous rooms from the former home of the Buquoy family, originally from Flanders.

### **11 Ego Dekor**★

Maltézské nám., 12
☎ 99 53 621
Open Mon.-Fri. 11am-7pm,
Sat. 11am-7.30pm, Sun.
11.30am-6.30pm.

Jiří Šemečků has added his own very creative touch to the crafts of glassblowing and wrought iron work. His shop contains stunning and refreshingly original items, including candle-holders, lights, frames and other unusual gift ideas. You can have large pieces, such as beds and tables, delivered anywhere in the world. This is a great place to buy gifts to take home.

## ⓬ U Vladaře★

Maltézské nám., 10
☎ 57 53 61 21
Open every day noon-1am.

On your left is a welcoming restaurant, which you'll no doubt be encouraged to try out. Be strong, resist and enter the tavern on the right instead. Here you'll dine in an equestrian setting, complete with stagecoach lamps, and be served delicious Czech dishes. This is the perfect opportunity to try dumplings (knedlíky, see p. 28).

## ⓭ Bar Bar★

Všehrdova, 17
☎ 53 29 41
Open every day noon-midnight

This restaurant is in an old vaulted cellar with yellow walls. It's run by an authentic descendant of one of the great

Czech families, who worked at the Jalta Hotel for many years before the Velvet Revolution. Order one of their enormous salads or pancakes, and Count

Antonín Kinský will be at your service all evening.

## ⓮ Kampa Island (Kampa)★★

Kampa is the largest of the islands in the Vltava and is formed by a branch of the river known as the Devil's Stream (Čertovka). It's said to be

## ⓯ THE THREE OSTRICHES (U TŘÍ PŠTROSŮ)★★

Dražického nám., 12
☎ 57 32 05 65
Restaurant open every day noon-3pm, 6-11pm.

The three ostriches on the front wall of the hotel were originally painted in the 17th century by Master Jan Fux, supplier of ostrich feathers to the court. The rooms are small, noisy and expensive. Do try and take a look at their painted wood Renaissance ceilings or at the exquisite ceiling in the small restaurant. Here you can enjoy a traditional meal in elegant surroundings. Choose from carp, goulash and a large selection of beef dishes.

haunted by evil spirits. There are three old mills on the island and the restored wheel of the Grand Prior's Mill. It has become known as the 'Venice of Prague', but with the occasional canoe instead of gondolas. It was once home to several artists, including the composer Bohuslav Martinů and the poet Vítězslav Nezval. The oval main square, Na Kampě, has some lovely 17th-century houses around it.

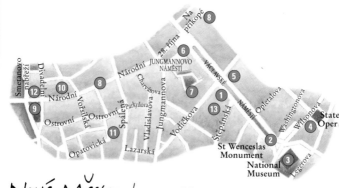

# Nové Město, the New Town

The New Town was founded in 1348 by Charles IV, after the Old Town had become too cramped. Nowadays, the 'golden triangle', formed by Národní and Na příkopě streets with Wenceslas Square, is an important centre for commerce, cafés and casinos. Once a horse market, it's now full of hotels, restaurants and shops. It's a hive of activity during the day, and at night the music from the clubs spills out onto the pavements. At all hours and in all weather, you'll see people strolling between stalls on Wenceslas Square and tasting the sizzling *párek* (sausages served with sweet and sour mustard and chunks of bread).

## ❶ Wenceslas Square (Václavské náměstí)★★

In its medieval days, Wenceslas Square was a horse market. Today it's a wide boulevard, partly pedestrianised, and Prague's own Champs-Elysées. It was here that independence was declared in 1918, that the Nazi occupation was challenged in 1938 and that the huge spontaneous demonstrations took place before the Velvet Revolution in November 1989.

## ❷ Wenceslas Monument★

Near the equestrian statue of St Wenceslas, the focal point of the uprisings against the Communist regime in 1968 and 1989, is a small plaque commemorating the victims of Communism from 1948-89.

It also serves as a memorial to the student Jan Palach, who set himself on fire on 16 January 1969, as a protest against the Russian occupation.

### ❸ National Museum⋆

Wenceslas Square, 68
☎ 24 49 71 11
Open every day exc. Tue. 9am-5pm
Entry charge.

The museum was completed in 1890 and dominates Wenceslas Square as a rather pompous statement of nationalism. Its dusty natural history collections contrast awkwardly with the kitsch splendour of its Pantheon, containing busts and statues of Czech scholars, writers and artists.

### ❹ State Opera (Státní Opera)⋆

Wilsonova, 4
☎ 24 22 76 93

The building opened in 1888 as the New German Theatre and was intended to be a rival to the magnificent Czech National Theatre (see p. 54), which had an exclusively Czech repertoire. It's a smaller replica of the Vienna Opera, but the adjacent freeway sadly spoils its neo-Classical façade.

### ❺ Europa Hotel Café⋆⋆⋆

Wenceslas Square, 25
☎ 24 22 81 17
Open every day 7am-7pm.

An Art Nouveau masterpiece, this café was completed in 1904 and is a compulsory stop on your itinerary. Its interior is rather shabby due to lack of repair, but the café has a wonderful middle European charm and a colourful clientèle. It's a reminder of the golden age of hotels, with its original bars, mirrors and panelling.

### ❻ Bata⋆

Wenceslas Square, 6
☎ 24 21 81 33
Open Mon.-Fri. 9am-9pm,
Sat. 9am-6pm, Sun. 10am-6pm

This famous Czech shoe brand name was established in 1894 and was finally restored in 1992 to its former owners, who had been in exile in Canada. The shoes remain the same as ever,

but the functional style of architecture is certainly worth a look. You may run into Tomáš Baťa, rightful heir to the empire, who began his working life here as a salesman in the 1930s.

## **7** Franciscan Garden (Františkánská zahrada)★

Jungmannovo nám., 18
Open every day 6am-7pm.

Just next to the Gothic St Mary-of-the-Snows Church (Panna Maria Snĕžká) is a haven of greenery and tranquillity. Originally the physic garden of a Franciscan monastery, elderly ladies come here to chat over an ice cream, and local workers have their lunch on the white wooden benches. The garden has been open to the public since 1950. Escape the bustle of Wenceslas Square and enjoy this oasis.

## **8** Národní třída and Na příkopĕ★

These two avenues followed the course of the Old Town moat until 1760, and they still mark the border between the Old and New Towns. Partly pedestrianised, they became the main promenades for the Czech and German bourgeoisie at the turn of the century. The boulevards are full of shops and restaurants, banks and clubs, but don't forget to have a look at Národní třída, 40. The 'Rondo-Cubist' architecture of the Adria Palace (1922-25) will take you by surprise. It was here that the first of Václav Havel's meetings of the civic forum took place in 1989.

## **9** National Theatre (Národní divadlo)★★

Národní, 2
☎ 24 91 26 73/24 91

The theatre is a proud symbol of the Czech national identity. It was financed entirely by private subscriptions but was destroyed by fire the year it was opened. A second patriotic donation of money made possible the reconstruction of this impressive neo-Renaissance building on the edge of the Vltava river. Completed in just two years, it's a powerful symbol in a country whose first elected president post Communism was a man of the theatre himself. The theatre was restored during the late 70s and Karel Prager built the New Stage.

## **10** Art Nouveau buildings – Praha and Topič★

Národní, 7 & 9

Osvald Polivka designed two
buildings in the Art Nouveau
style. It's interesting to
compare Praha and its
stunning mosaics inspired by
the Viennese Secession, with
Topič, whose much more
ostentatious facade was
influenced by the German
Jugendstil. Praha was built for
the Prague insurance company
of the same name. A modest
employee by the name of
Franz Kafka worked there for
several years (see p. 16).

## ⓫ Velryba★

Opatovická, 24
☎ 24 91 23 91/70 80
Open every day 11-2am.

If, like Jonah, you wander into
'The Whale', you'll have
discovered one of the best
cafés in Prague. It's one of the
increasingly popular 'gallery-

cafés'. Literary
and artistic locals
come to read their
papers on
splendid
mahogany tables
and to enjoy
good food at
reasonable
prices,
including a
selection of
vegetarian
dishes.
Those in the
know go
straight to
the back
room, which
is more
comfortable
with its low tables and
welcoming chairs.

## ⓬ Café Slavia★★

Národní, 1
☎ 24 22 09 57
Open every day 9am-11pm.

This is one of the most
mythical cafés in Central
Europe, with huge picture
windows and panoramic views
of the Castle. It was closed in
1992, an event which gave rise
to many indignant petitions.
Six years later it opened its
doors again, having been
tastefully renovated. It's the
old friend of dissidents and

## ⓭ LUCERNA (PALÁC LUCERNA)★

Access via Štěpánská, 61 or
Vodičkova, 36.

In the 20s, Václav Havel's
grandfather designed
Prague's most famous
arcade in Moorish style.
The Lucerna Palace is
enormous and houses cafés,
restaurants, shops, a cinema,
a night club and a ballroom.
The traditional graduation
dances are held here (see
p. 27), and a famous jazz
festival, held since 1964,
takes place in October,
attracting international
musicians. The locals
continue to watch with
interest the progress of the
Havel family dispute over
the building.

artists, and once more the
favourite haunt of Prague's
intelligentsia. They serve
a strong but
quite legal
absinthe,
whose
inebriating
powers need
to be
treated
with the
greatest
respect.

# Petřín, Lover's Hill

If you're in a romantic mood, take a walk on the wooded slopes of Petřín hill. The southern side was planted with vineyards in the 12th century, but by the 18th century these had been transformed into gardens and orchards. It's a perfect spot for a romantic stroll, and the local tradition is for lovers to embrace in front of the monument to Karel Hynek Mácha, the most famous Czech Romantic poet, who died in 1836 at the age of 26.

### ❶ Petřín Park (Petřínksé Sady)★★

Access by funicular railway.
Open every day 9.15am-9.45pm.

Jump on the funicular (*U Lanová dráhy*, Ujezd St.) and you'll soon find yourself on the rooftop of Prague.

The Observation Tower and the Church of St Lawrence are at the summit, together with two relics from the 1891 Jubilee Exhibition. Try navigating The Mirror Maze and climbing the scaled-down version of the Eiffel Tower, with 299 steps and no lift. From the tower, weather permitting, you should be able to see Bohemia's highest peak in the Giant Mountains, known as Sněžka.

### ❷ Hunger Wall (Hladová zed)★

The remains of almost 1,200 m/1,300 yds of crenellated fortifications run from Ujezd to Strahov across Petřín Park. Built in 1360-62, the wall takes its name from a decision made by Charles IV to order the construction of a huge wall as

employment for the poor and wretched victims of a dreadful famine. The battlements are also said by some to resemble teeth.

### ❸ Vlašská Street★

The most picturesque way to descend from Petřín is to take the 'Italian street', so called

because of the immigrants who settled there to rebuild the Castle in the 16th century. The grandest building is Lobkowicz Palace, now the German embassy. It's one of the finest Baroque palaces, built by the Italian Alliprandi at the beginning of the 18th century. It's best viewed from the rear but sadly the magnificent gardens are no longer open to the public.

## ❹ Vrtbov Gardens (Vrtbovská Zahrada)★★

Karmelitská, 25

This beautiful Baroque garden lies behind Vrtbov Palace and has magnificent views. The statues of Classical gods and stone vases were sculpted by Matthias Braun, whilst the garden itself was designed by Franktišek Maximilián Kaňka in about 1720.

## ❺ Nebozízek Restaurant★★

Petřínské Sady, 411
☎ 551 017
Open every day 11am-11pm.

This restaurant is worth a detour for its unbeatable view. It takes its name from the winding path up the hill which you take to reach it.

Alternatively, you can walk from the funicular station halfway up the hill. The view is much more spectacular than the food.

## ❻ Michna Palace (Michnův Palác)★

Újezd, 40
☎ 532 116

Open Tue.-Sat. 9am-5pm,
Sun 10am-5pm
Entry charge.

This elegant Baroque palace on the site of an old Dominican convent was the summer residence of the aristocratic Kinský family. It is now the home of the university's sports faculty and, on the ground floor, the Museum of Physical Culture and Sport. A physical culture association, Sokol, bought the palace in 1921 and converted it into a sports centre. It was

## ❼ Church of St Mary the Victorious (Panna Maria Vitezna)★★

Karmelitská, 9
Open every day, 8.30am-3.30pm.

Prague's first Baroque church houses the Bambino di Praga, a wax effigy of the infant Jesus brought from Spain in the 15th century and attributed with miraculous powers. The effigy has an extensive wardrobe, which comprises over 60 different coats. One of the coats was sewn by Maria Theresa of Austria herself in gratitude for protecting the city during the French occupation in 1742. The effigy also has a record of miracle cures.

renamed Tyrš House in honour of Sokol's founder, Miroslav Tyrš.

# Staré Město, the Old Town and its little streets

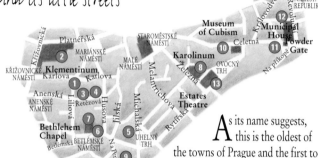

As its name suggests, this is the oldest of the towns of Prague and the first to achieve this status and accompanying privileges in about 1230, when Prague found itself at the crossroads of central European trade routes. This is where the Prague of labyrinthine medieval passages and alleyways begins and many of Pragues busiest restaurants and shops are to be found here. You'll enjoy soaking up the atmosphere in these narrow old streets at the heart of the city.

## ❶ Charles Street (Karlova ulice)★★

This narrow, winding street dates back to the 12th century and links Charles Bridge and Old Town Square. Its many shops sell mainly souvenirs, glassware and wooden toys. Follow the Royal Route, along which kings and queens of Bohemia passed on their way to their coronation at St Vitus's Cathedral. Watch out for the Renaissance house and the French Crown (no. 4), where Kepler drew up the laws carrying his name on the movement of planets in 1607-12. Prague's first café was established in 1714 at the House of the Golden Snake (no. 18).

## ❷ Klementinum★★
Křižovnické nám. 4
☎ 21 66 33 31

The largest group of buildings after the Castle, the Klementinum was founded in 1556 by the Jesuits, who were commissioned to bring the Czechs back into the Catholic fold and became the headquarters of the Counter Reformation. Sadly, the wonderful library is closed

to the public, but you can attend a concert in the beautiful Chapel of Mirrors (Zrcadlová Kaple), said by some to resemble a boudoir rather than a sacred place. Its interior is decorated with fake marble and mirror panels and it has excellent acoustics.

## ❸ House of the Lords of Kunštát★

Řetězová, 3
☎ 0602 220 698
Open Tue.-Sun. 11am-6pm.

To avoid flooding, the level of this house has been raised, and in the basement there are three of Prague's best-preserved Romanesque rooms. The Lord of Kunstat offered his home to his nephew George of Podebrady, future king of Bohemia, in the 15th century. A permanent exhibition traces the life of this moderate Hussite king in the beautiful Romanesque suite.

## ❹ At the Golden Tiger (U Zlatého tygra)★★

Husova, 17
☎ 22 22 11 11
Open every day 3-11pm.
The Golden Tiger has become a bit of a cult pub, where the late writer Bohumil Hrabal came to find inspiration. He died in 1997 at the age of 83. Don't be intimidated by

the predominantly male clientèle, most of whom will be locals. They'll move up to fit you in at the long tables. Order a Pilsen and you'll be instantly accepted.

## ❺ Vinárna Blatnička★

Michalská, 5
Open every day 11am-midnight.

This is a lively wine bar, which is always busy and only sells local produce from the Blatnicka co-operative in

South Moravia. If you find yourself hesitating between a Vavřinecké and a Riesling, ask Zdeněk what he would suggest. His Moravian hospitality will transcend any language barriers that may exist.

## ❻ Architects Club (Klub architektů)★

Betlémské nám., 5a
☎ 24 40 12 14
Open every day 11.30am-midnight.

This restaurant is run by the Institute of Architects and is a favourite haunt of artists and intellectuals. In the summer you can enjoy candles on the terrace

overlooking the Bethlehem Chapel. Booking is essential.

## ❼ Bethlehem Chapel (Betlémská Kaple)★

Betlémské nám.
Open every day 9am-6pm (5pm Nov.-Mar.)
Entry charge.

Although this chapel is a faithful reconstruction, completed by Jarosla Frágner after the Second World War, you'll be treading on the same ground as the famous reformer, Jan Hus. He delivered his passionate sermons against the Church and the Pope between 1402-12. This is the place to visit if you're keen to learn more about the Hussites.

### **8** Karolinum★

Železná, 9
☎ 24 49 16 32
Closed to the public.

Charles IV founded Central
Europe's first university here
in 1348, determined to make
Prague the political and
cultural centre of Europe.

Today this ancient Baroque
building is the administrative
core of the Charles University.
It has a few beautiful Gothic
touches, which are at their
best when viewed from the
corner of Železná and
Ovocný trh.

### **9** Antique Glass Gallery 'A' ★★

Na Perštýně, 10
☎ 26 13 34
Open every day 11am-7pm.

You're likely to fall in love
with the Cubist furniture and
lights at this gallery. If not,
then the stunning ceilings,
painted in the 1920s, will
capture your heart. If the
prices for the glassware,
ranging from 18th century to
the Art Deco period, are too
high for you (though justified),
then settle for lovely copies of
medieval, Gothic or Baroque
glass. There's a small
exhibition room, where
original work from

contemporary artists,
including Klinger and
Masitova is on display.

### **10** Museum of Cubism ★★

Celetná, 34
☎ 24 21 17 32
Open every day exc. Mon.
10am-6pm.

Josef Gočár erected this
controversial building in 1912.
It was formerly a Baroque
residence but only the
symbolic statue of the black
Virgin remained after its
reconstruction, hence its name
'House of the Black Virgin'.
The key exponents of the
Czech Cubist movement are
exhibited here, including Otto
Guttfreund, Josef Chochol
and Emil Filla.

### **11** Powder Tower (Prašná Brána)★

Nám. Republiky
Open every day 10am-6pm
(5pm Apr.-Oct. Closed
Nov.-Mar.).

The tower acquired its name
when it was used to store
gunpowder in the 17th century.
It's now a museum, housing
exhibitions on Prague's towers.

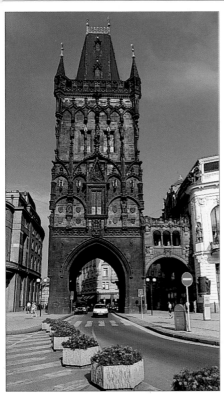

### **®** ESTATES THEATRE (STAVOVSKÉ DIVADLO)★★

Ovocný trh, 6
☎ 24 21 50 01.

On 29 October 1787, Mozart's *Don Giovanni* had its debut here with the composer himself at the piano. It was an historic performance, made even more remarkable by the fact that Mozart had composed his famous overture in D minor only two days before. The theatre itself is one of the finest examples of neo-Classical architecture in Prague.

Much more impressive, however, is the magnificent view over a sea of grey-green domes and tiled roofs which is well worth the climb up this vestige of the Old Town's few remaining ramparts.

### ⑫ Municpal House (Obecní Dům)★★★

Nám. Republiky, 5
☎ 22 00 21 00
Open Mon.-Sat. 10am-6pm.

This delightful Art Nouveau building, lovingly restored and a mecca for enthusiasts of this architectural style, was designed by Antonin Balšánek and Osvald Polívka (1905-1911). Works by Alfons

Mucha decorate the interior, alongside those of other leading Czech artists from the first decade of the twentieth century. It houses a selection of venues: a French brasserie, a splendid Viennese-style café,

the Plzeňská restaurant, the Smetana concert hall and a piano-bar, where you can dance from 6pm until midnight on Saturdays and Sundays.

# Staroměstské náměstí,
## the Old Town Square

The Old Town Hall is one of Prague's most striking buildings. Originally established in 1338, it has expanded over the centuries and now consists of a row of colourful Gothic and Renaissance buildings. After serious damage by the Nazis in the 1945 Prague Uprising, most of these buildings were restored.

The Old Town Square itself is the traditional heart of the city, full of cafés, restaurants, shops and, of course, tourists.

### ❶ Old Town Square (Staroměstské náměstí)★★★

This is the oldest market in the town, dating back to 1091, and is a perfect venue for an open air lesson in Czech history. You'll see 27 white crosses set into the paving, which symbolise the Protestants executed in 1621 following the Battle of the White Mountain. It was after this that the country fell into the hands of the Habsburgs. Klement Gottwald proclaimed the Communist state in the town square in 1948, and Václav Havel announced the return to democracy in the same square 42 years later.

### ❷ Jan Hus Monument★

Ladislas Šaloun's Art Nouveau monument to Jan Hus was unveiled on the 500th anniversary of the reformer's death. He was burnt alive in 1415 after being pronounced a heretic. This massive symbol of national identity is also a popular meeting place.

### ❸ Old Town Hall (Staroměstská Radnice)★★★

Staroměstské nám., 3
Open Mon. 11am–6pm, Tue.–Sun. 9am–6pm (5pm, Oct.–Mar.).

The astronomical clock (1410) is the town hall's main attraction. On the hour, a crowd of tourists and locals gathers to watch the procession of clock figures depicting Christ, followed by his Apostles, while a skeleton

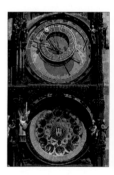

pulls on the rope to ring a bell. Climb up the tower for a unique view of the city.

### ❹ Church of Our Lady Before Týn (Kostel Panny Marie Před Týnem)★★

Staroměstské nám., 14
Under reconstruction.

This dark Gothic church (1365) was the most important of the Hussite churches built

in Prague. Its steeples dominate the square, and it houses the tomb of the Danish astronomer Tycho Brahé, who died of a burst bladder during a royal audience with Rudolph II. Not wanting to 'die like Tycho Brahé' is a colloquialism for needing to go to the toilet.

## ❺ The Small Square (Malé náměstí)★★

Prague's first apothecary opened in 1353 on this delightful extension of the Old Town Square. The Lékarná Schöblingová (no. 13) has a beautiful Baroque interior, almost completely preserved. Take a look inside and don't miss the lovely Renaissance fountain.

## ❻ Church of St Nicolas (Kostel Sv Mikuláše)★

Staroměstské nám., 14
Open Tue.-Sun. 10am-5pm.

The present church by Ignaz Dientzenhofer was completed in 1735, though there's been a church on this site since the 12th century. It looks rather like a giant wedding cake with its white façade studded with statues. Don't miss the enormous Bohemian chandelier.

## ❼ Týn courtyard★★

The courtyard is better known by its German name Ungelt, meaning 'no money', which was meant to deter invaders. Between the 11th and 18th centuries foreign merchants were housed here, and it became a successful international marketplace. Look out for the Granovský house, recognisable by its elegant first floor open loggia. Built in 1560 according to the model for an Italian Renaissance palace, its sgraffito frescoes show scenes from the Bible and mythology.

## ❽ Café Milena★

Staroměstské nám., 22
☎ 21 63 26 02
Open every day 10am-8pm.

Located on the first floor of the Kafka centre (see p. 16), this café was named after his lover Milena Jesenská. It's difficult to tell if the elegant elderly ladies who frequent the café come to enjoy the wonderful cream pastries or to watch people go by in the Old Town Square below.

## ❾ ROTT CRYSTAL★

Malé nám., 3
☎ (and fax) 26 95 37
Open Mon.-Fri. 7.30am-7pm,
Sat. 9.30am-7pm,
Sun. 10am-6pm.

You can still read the name of the first owner on the neo-Renaissance facade of the most famous shop in the city. Rott was also responsible for the construction of the Prague metro. This former ironmonger's shop was decorated by the painter Mikuláš Aleš and has been converted into a store selling high-quality crystalware on several floors.

# Vyšehrad, the castle on the heights

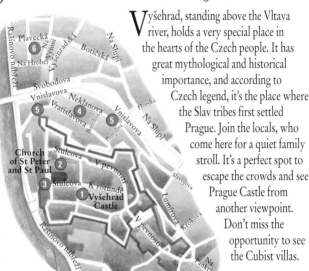

Vyšehrad, standing above the Vltava river, holds a very special place in the hearts of the Czech people. It has great mythological and historical importance, and according to Czech legend, it's the place where the Slav tribes first settled Prague. Join the locals, who come here for a quiet family stroll. It's a perfect spot to escape the crowds and see Prague Castle from another viewpoint. Don't miss the opportunity to see the Cubist villas.

## ❶ Vyšehrad Castle★★

Entry via Pevnosti Street.

Vratislav II, first king of Bohemia, founded the castle in the 11th century, but it was later superseded by Prague Castle, which was easier to defend. Abandoned after its

destruction during the Hussite wars, it was then transformed into a powerful fortress in the 17th century. The restored St Martin's rotunda is the sole survivor of the medieval fortress. Vyšehrad is now a symbol of Czech nationhood.

## ❷ Vyšehrad Cemetery (Vyšehradsky hřbitov)★★

Open every day 8am-7pm (9am-4pm Nov.-Feb., 8am-6pm Mar.-Apr.)

As a tribute to the role they played in the foundation of the nation, the grateful citizens gave this cemetery over to the key artists and intellectuals involved. Buried here are the authors Jan Neruda, Vítězslav Nezval and Karel Čapek

(famous as the inventor of the word 'robot'), together with the composers Bedřich Smetana and Antonín Dvořák, whose memorial is very elaborate with a mosaic inscription. The painter Alfons Mucha also rests in the cemetery, which was founded in 1869.

## ❸ Church of St Peter and St Paul★★

Open Sat.-Sun. 10am-noon, 1-4pm.

Josef Mocker built this neo-Gothic church in 1885 on the foundations of the 11th-century basilica, commissioned by Vratislav II. In the adjoining garden there are four statues of legendary figures from Czech mythology by Josef Myslbek.

## ❹ The Golden Anchor (U zlaté kotvy)★

Vratislavova, 19
☎ 90 05 20 21
Open every day 10am-midnight.

As the name suggests, the interior of this beer hall has a marine theme. Fishing nets hang in the windows and the bar is shaped like a ship's prow. Excellent beer is served, but do remember that you're in a

landlocked country when choosing your meal. Avoid the frozen fish dishes and opt instead for the rustic Czech specialities, such as *bramborák*, which is a delicious potato pancake.

## ❺ Czech Cubism★★★

The villas in Vyšehrad were all built between 1911 and 1913 in the Cubist style that was very popular in Prague at the time. Take a tour of the buildings, beginning at Neklanova, 30, with Josef Chochol's impressive structure. Notice the door handles but avoid the restaurant inside. Further along at no. 2, you'll be able to admire Antonín Belada's Cubist façade. Finish off your walk with a visit to two more of Chochol's works. At Libušina, 49, look at his cleverly designed triangular garden, and at Rašínovo ná břeži, 6, 8 and 10 cast your eye over the elegant house he designed, which is large enough for three families.

## ❻ Le Bistrot de Marlène ★★

Plavecká, 4
☎ 29 10 77
Open Mon.-Fri. noon-2.30pm, 7.30-10.15pm, Sat. 7-10.30pm

This is a lovely, exotic restaurant far from the madding crowd. The bubbly

## ❼ THE LEGEND OF PRINCESS LIBUŠE

Princess Libuše is said to have prophesied the future glory of Prague from the top of Vyšehrad. From 710 she ruled over a people reluctant to be led by a woman. They soon demanded that she took a husband. Libuše chose a man called Přemysl (meaning ploughman) and founded the Přemyslid dynasty, which ruled over Bohemia until the 14th century.

French maître d'hôtel, Marlène, has been in Prague since 1995 and has taken no time at all to convince her Czech customers that there's gastronomic life beyond the traditional roast pork and dumplings.

# Rooms and Restaurants

Hotels in Prague are generally expensive. The renovated hotels are both smart and pricey, whereas good budget accommodation is more difficult to find. *Pensions* are a recent alternative and are smaller and less expensive, but the standard can vary dramatically. In restaurants and cafes, don't be surprised to find people eating their meals in crowded rooms, elbow to elbow, and with unusual haste.

## HOTELS

There's little accommodation to be found in Prague between the four star hotel and the small *pension*. Accommodation is expensive, and you will find it hard to get a combination of cleanliness, great comfort and stylish decor all at the same time, even in the most expensive hotels. However, things are gradually improving as our selection demonstrates.

### CLASSIFICATION

There are three basic categories of accommodation: 'A' for rooms, suites and apartments in luxury hotels (from Kč2,500-4,000), 'B' for more standard hotels (from Kč1,500-2,000) and 'C' for smaller hotels and *pensions* (from Kč750-1,500). In the high season, from early May to late September, hotels put up their prices, which duly fall again in the low season. It is sometimes possible to negotiate rates.

### HOTEL RESERVATIONS

Demand for hotel rooms exceeds supply in Prague. If your travel package does not include a room, it's advisable to make a reservation by telephone or on the internet in advance, even in the less busy periods. During Easter, between July and August and at New Year, you should book your accommodation ahead.

## RESTAURANTS

The locals start work at 7-8am. They have a quick stand-up sandwich for lunch around noon, usually in a snack-bar or *hospoda*. The working day ends at 4-5pm with dinner over by 7pm. You can appreciate why it's difficult to get a meal after 9pm in a *hospoda* or after 10.30pm in a restaurant.

We strongly recommend that you make dinner reservations, even in the simplest *hospoda*, to avoid being disappointed or having to queue for a long time. To secure a table in the better-known restaurants, you need to book a few days ahead.

### CZECH ETIQUETTE

Czech diners tend to sit next to each other rather than opposite. You will often find yourself joining others at a table, but there's no obligation to enter into a conversation with your neighbours. It's customary to have your plate taken away as soon as you've finished your meal, even if your fellow diners are still in the middle of eating. In order to slow down the service a little, cross your knife and fork on your plate to indicate that you haven't finished yet. Put them both to one side when you wish for your plate to be taken away. This isn't

## LAST MINUTE ACCOMODATION

**Tourtip Viviane**
Cukrovarnická, 22,
Prague 6 - Střešovice
☎ 24 31 13 61 📠 24 31 13 59
mobile: 0602 851 951
tourtip@centrum.cz
If you arrive in Prague with
no accommodation, you'd
be wise to call Tourtip.
They'll come up with a wide
selection of hotels in
different categories. Payment
is accepted in cash only, and
the staff speak English.

**Tom's Travel**
Ostrovní, 7, Prague 1
☎ 24 99 09 00
info@apartments.cz
www.apartments.cz
Open every day 8am-8pm.
Whether you need a room,
a suite, a *pension* or an
apartment, Tom's Travel will
send a selection by fax, mail
or e-mail according to your
budget and requirements.
They'll supply photos and
maps even at the last minute
and the staff speak English.

**Athos Travel**
Na Strzi, 5, Prague 4
☎ 24 14 40 571 📠 24 14 46 97
info@athos.cz
www.athos.cz
Athos can arrange rooms, car
rental, tours and transfer from
the airport (Kč550 for up to
4 people). Staff are efficient,
friendly and speak English.

guaranteed to work every
time though! A glass of soda
water (*soda*) or mineral water
(*mineralka*) will sometimes
be brought to the table.

In some establishments your
beer will be replaced
automatically once your glass

is empty. Don't hesitate to
refuse, even if there is some
pressure to continue drinking.

## PAYMENT AND TIPS

When the bill arrives, check it
carefully. You may find that an
extra cover charge or a charge
for the bread has been added.
A main meal won't usually
include vegetables or rice.
When you're ready to pay, add
a tip of 5-10% to the bill, tell
this to the waiter and it will be
deducted as a tip from your
change. Don't leave the money
on the table though. For a
quick meal in a *hospoda* you
will pay Kč60-100. A meal in
a more up-market restaurant
will cost around Kč500.

## VEGETARIANS

Restaurant menus do feature
dishes without meat (*jidla bez
masa*). However, this does not
necessarily mean that they are
lighter. You could try the
dumplings with scrambled egg
(*knedlíky s vejce*), the crumbed
and fried cheese (*smažený sýr*)
or mushrooms (*smažené
žampióny*). It's worth tasting
the tofu dishes (*sojové maso*).

Some vegetarian restaurants
worth trying are:
Country Life (see p. 72),
Radost Fx (see p.
120) and Govinda
(see Staying On
section at the
back of the
book)

You may find
the following
phrases useful:
'jsem vegetarián/
vegetariánka'
(I am a vegetarian);

'nejím maso nebo ryby'
(I don't eat meat or fish).
(See p. 121 for more handy
words and phrases.)

## PLACES TO EAT

*Samoobsluha*
These are self-service snack-
bars with minimal seating,
where you can have great-value
hot meals. They're usually
non-smoking.

*Pivnice, hospoda, hostinec*
These are all pubs, where
you'll find that most Czechs
go to eat and drink.

*Vinárna*
You may be able to have a
snack in these popular wine
bars.

*Restaurace*
This is the equivalent of a
restaurant, though the menu
here may differ little from
that of a *hospoda*.

*Cukrárna*
Try the delicious pastries at
these cafes – they're great value!
A croissant (*loupák*) will cost
Kč12. The traditional pastry is
known as *koláč* and is served
with plum jam (*povidlový*)

or poppy
seed jam
(*makový*).

# HOTELS

## Malá Strana

### Hotel Kampa ★★
Všehrdova 16,
Prague 1
☎ 57 32 05 08
🅕 57 32 02 62
Trams 12 or 22, Újezd station
Double room low season
Kč3,860, high season Kč4,680,
inc. breakfast.

Wonderfully located in a peaceful side street, this 17th-century Baroque building was a former armoury. The hotel was renovated in 1922 and has 85 rooms with shower. Some have lovely views over Kampa Park and the river. The restaurant is open 7am-10pm. On sunny days you can

sit out on the terrace and enjoy a relaxing drink or meal.

### Hotel Sax
Jánský vršek 3, Prague 1
☎ 57 53 01 72
🅕 53 84 98
Trams 12, 22, Malostranské
Square stop
Double room Kč4,400.

This hotel is located in a street that runs parallel with Nerudova, as it leads up to the Castle. At the end of the day, you'll have the area to yourself. The bar and restaurant are open from 11.30am-10pm.

### Pension Dientzenhofer ★★
Nosticova 2, Prague 1
☎ 53 88 96/53 16 72
🅕 53 71 08 88
Trams 12, 22, Malostranské
Square stop
Double room Kč3,500.

The architect Kilian Dientzenhofer was born in this 15th-century building, which has only six rooms, so you do need to book well in advance. Situated near Charles Bridge, it's in a quiet residential area, and in summer you can have breakfast in the garden overlooking the lovely Kampa Park.

### Pension U raka
Černínská 10, Prague 1
☎ 20 51 11 00
🅕 20 51 05 11
Tram 22
Double room Kč6,200.

Located in the Nový Svět district, this *pension* is housed

in a half-timbered house. The seven rooms are comfortable, and you'll have a quiet stay – children and dogs aren't allowed.

## The Peacock Hotel (U Páva)★★★★

U Lužického semináře 32, Prague 1
☎ 57 32 07 43
🖷 53 33 79
Trams 12, 22, Malostranské Square stop
Metro Malostranská
Double room Kč5,900, inc. breakfast.

This charming hotel is situated almost on the banks of the Vltava near the Charles Bridge, which makes it quite expensive. It has a wonderful view of the Castle and a restaurant with excellent fish dishes. The rooms are comfortable and spacious.

## Hotel Hoffmeister★★★★

Pod Bruskou 9, Prague 1
☎ 51 01 71 11
Metro Malostranská
Double room Kč7,000.

This is a large, modern luxury hotel was designed by the son of Adolf Hoffmeister, a friend of Picasso and the French Surrealists. The 43 rooms are tastefully decorated and well worth the extra cost, if this is the sort of accommodation you're looking for.

## Na Kampě 15★★

Na Kampě 15, Prague 1
Trams 12, 22, Malostranské Square stop
☎ 57 31 89 96
🖷 57 31 89 97
Double room Kč4,000-5,800.

This former 15th-century brewery on the island of Kampa in the Vltava is a listed building that has now been converted into a marvellous riverside hotel. It has a number of rooms under the eaves, a restaurant with a small garden and an old-fashioned beer room.

## Staré Město

### Betlém Club

Betlémské nám. 9, Prague 1
☎ 22 22 15 75
Metro Národní třída
Double room Kč3,600.

Ideally situated on Bethlehem Square near several cafés and restaurants, this *pension* has 20 small rooms at reasonable prices. Enjoy your breakfast in an authentic Gothic cellar.

## Grand Hotel Europa★★★

Wenceslas Square, 25, Prague 1
☎ 24 22 81 17
🖷 24 22 45 44
Metro Mustek or Muzeum
Double room Kč3,740.

The Europa is a beautiful hotel with Art Nouveau decoration. It has all the antiquated charm of a turn of the century hotel, though some of the rooms were recently renovated. There's some stunning glasswork in the dining room and the hotel's café is renowned throughout Prague and beyond. The service isn't quite up to the standard you might expect from a hotel in this category, but the prices take this into account.

Havel was once held in cell number 6 in the basement. It's now a peaceful *pension* where you'll find yourself in the quiet company of the Franciscan sisters.

### The Goldsmith's Hotel (Hotel U Klenotníka)
Rytířská 3, Prague 1
☎ 24 21 16 99
🖷 24 22 10 25
Metro Můstek
Double room Kč3,800.

Conveniently located between Wenceslas Square and the Old Town Square, this family-run pension has a lovely restaurant and ten very comfortable rooms. In former years it was a jewellery factory .

### King George Pension (Pension U Krále Jiřího)
Liliová 10, Prague 1
☎ 22 22 17 07
🖷 22 22 17 07
Metro Staromestská
Double room Kč2,600.

This 14th-century building has only eight rooms, some located in the attic. It is simply decorated and its greatest attribute is its central location near Charles Bridge.

### Hotel Esprit★★★
Jakubská 5, Prague 1
☎ 22 87 01 11
🖷 22 87 01 12
Metro nám. Republiky
Double room Kč5,400–6,400.

Hospitality is the watchword of this Art Deco hotel, located near the Municipal House. Now entirely renovated, it boasts 24 rooms (one of which has been adapted for handicapped guests), a conference room which overlooks the neighbouring

rooftops, a restaurant, a small garden, a nearby car park and even a limousine.

### U Staré paní
Michalská 9, Prague 1
☎ 26 72 67/26 49 20/ 26 16 55
Metro Můstek
Double room Kč3,830 in high season.

This hotel is ideally located and has recently been renovated. It has 18 clean, comfortable rooms, and the jazz club in the basement has an excellent programme.

### Pension Unitas
Bartolomějská 9, Prague 1
☎ 24 21 10 20
🖷 24 21 08 00
Metro Národní třída
Double room Kč2,000.

This house used to be a Jesuit monastery and then a prison for political prisoners, where the secret police conducted their interrogations. Václav

### Hotel Černa Liska★★
U radnice 16/19, Prague 1
☎ 90 00 40 66
🖷 90 00 40 33
Metro Staroměstská
Double room Kč3,100–4,800.

You couldn't find anywhere nearer the heart of the Old Town to stay than in this charming hotel which overlooks Staroměstská Square. Its 12 renovated rooms provide comfortable accommodation, and in fine weather breakfast is served on the terrace overlooking the square.

reasonable prices, which are all extremely clean if a touch small. Recently renovated, the hotel is in excellent condition and has a simple but attractive decor.

### Pension City
Belgická 10
☎ 22 52 16 06
Metro nám. Míru
Double room Kč2,320 with bathroom, Kč1,500 without.

This hotel is situated within a quiet leafy locale close to Nám. Míru, an attractive square with a lovely garden surrounded by interesting and colourful buildings. The rooms are small but clean, and excellent value.

## Further Afield

### Pension Bonaparte
Radlická 38, Prague 5
☎ 54 38 09
🖷 51 56 22 82
Metro Andél
Double room Kč2,000.

## Nové Město

### Hotel 16. U sv Kateřiny★★★
Kateřinská 16, Prague 2
☎ 24 91 96 76
🖷 24 91 06 26
Metro Karlovo náměstí
Double room Kč3,100, including breakfast.

Just a ten minute walk from Wenceslas Square and close to the Botanical Gardens, this hotel is in an ideal location. It has been entirely renovated and has suites, double rooms and single rooms, one of which has facilities for the disabled. All the rooms are quiet and comfortable, and some have small lounges to relax in at the end of the day.

## Vinohrady

### Hotel Anna
Budečská 17, Prague 2
☎ 22 51 31 11
🖷 22 51 51 58
Metro nám. Míru
Double room Kč3,000.

This hotel has 23 single and double rooms and is in a quiet area, close to the centre. The hotel has a bar with a terrace open from 5-11pm.

### Luník
Londýnská 50, Prague 2
☎ 24 25 39 74
🖷 24 25 39 86
Metro I.P. Pavlova
Double room Kč2,490.

This is a modernised hotel in a good location, just 15 minutes' walk or two metro stops from Wenceslas Square. There are 35 quiet rooms at

This *pension* is slightly out of the way, but it's only a ten minute walk from Můstek metro station and has a tram stop just opposite. The 19th-century house has been completely restored and has nine large, clean double rooms and an apartment catering for three people.

# RESTAURANTS

## Malá Strana

### Hanavský pavilon★
Letenské sady, 173
☎ 33 32 36 41
Trams 18 or 22, Chotkovy
sady stop, then Gogolova St.
to Letná Park
Open every day 11.30am-
3.30pm, 6pm-1am.

Situated in Letná Park, this
restaurant is decorated in the
Baroque and Rococo styles and
resembles a hunting lodge. The
view of Prague is magnificent,
the atmosphere peaceful and
the service extremely attentive.

### U černého vola★★
Lorétánské náměstí, 1
☎ 20 51 11 40
Tram 22, Pražský hrad stop
Open every day 10am-10pm.

Located next to Loreta church
and opposite the Ministry of
Foreign Affairs, this Baroque
house is home to an old inn,
which isn't yet on the tourist
map. On the menu are delicious
soups and simple dishes, which
you can wash down with a glass
of Velkopopovický Kozel beer.

### U Kocoura★★
Nerudova, 2
☎ 57 53 01 07
Trams 12, 22, Malostranské
nám. stop
Open every day 10am-11pm.

This is the place to taste the best
Pilsner Urquell beer in Prague
while enjoying local dishes of
sausages and cheese specially
concocted to complement the
beer.

### U Maltézských rytíru★★★
Prokopská, 10
☎ 53 63 57
Trams 12, 22, Malostranské
nám. stop
Open every day 11am-11pm.

Dine by candlelight in this
intimate restaurant close to the
French embassy. Choose a table
on the ground floor or in the
Romanesque basement. The
food is good value, with a
choice of local and international
dishes. Make sure you try the
apple strudel (jablkovy zavin).

## Staré Město

### Pivnice Radegast★
Templová, 2
☎ 23 28 069
Metro nám. Republiky
or Můstek
Open every
day 11am-
12.30am.

This busy
pub has
a lively
feel, with
the staff
continually
rushing around
re-filling beer glasses.
Try a dish of beef in cream sauce
(svíčková na smetaně) or a bowl
of goulash (guláš).

### Country Life★★
Melantrichova, 15
Metro Můstek
Open Mon.-Thu. 8am-7pm,
Fri. 8am-4pm, Sun. 11am-
6pm.

This is a great restaurant for
vegetarians and vegans, tucked

away in a pretty courtyard,
in fact at one time it was
almost Prague's only vegetarian restaurant. The salads,
soups, hot dishes and desserts,
all with Eastern European
touches are delicious. Don't
miss the beetroot soup (borsc).

### U Zlatého soudku★
Ostrovní, 28
☎ 24 91 22 03
Metro Národní třída
Open Mon.-Sat. 11am-11pm.

Seated in a green wooden
cubicle, you'll enjoy a choice of
traditional Czech dishes, served
in large, reasonably-priced portions and leave well satisfied. An
excellent choice on a chilly day.

### L'Equinoxe★
Vojtěšská, 9
☎ 29 10 40
Metro Národní třída
Open Mon.-Sat. noon-1am.

An excellent French restaurant
serving hot and cold salads, as
well as meat and fish dishes
(à la carte Kč100-300, set meal
Kč80). The café is open from
7am for an early continental
breakfast.

In the basement of the Municipal House there's a large *hospoda*, decorated with painted wood and ceramics. Choose from some delicious traditional dishes served in a warm, friendly atmosphere. You may be treated to a few strains of the accordion. This is one of the best examples of the *hospoda*.

### Vinárna v zátiší★★★
Liliová, 1
☎ 22 22 06 27
Metro Národní třída or Můstek
Open every day noon-3pm, 5.30-11pm.

If you're looking for the perfect place for a romantic meal, then look no further. Candlelit dinner in a sophisticated and peaceful atmosphere, with excellent and discreet service, is the order of the day. The dishes are original but inspired by Czech, French and international cuisines. The food is beautifully presented and wine can be bought by the glass. Bookings are needed in advance.

### Francouzská a Plzeňská restaurace★★★
Náměstí Republiky, 5
☎ 22 00 27 70
🖷 22 00 27 78
Metro nám. Republiky
Open every day noon-4pm, 6-11pm.

This wonderful Art Nouveau restaurant has an excellent selection of traditional Czech dishes together with some delicious French food. The prices are very reasonable and the atmosphere really welcoming. Treat yourself to a night out if you're only in Prague for a short time. Book in advance to avoid disappointment.

### Hospoda at the Municipal House★★
Náměstí Republiky, 5
☎ 22 00 27 80
Metro nám. Republiky
Open every day 11am-11pm.

### Pivnice u Pivrnce★
Maiselova, 3
☎ 23 29 40 41
Open every day 11am-11pm.

This pub is in the basement and is decorated with some amusing cartoons. You may well not appreciate the humour of the frescoes, which are rather saucy. The cuisine is simple and traditional, the atmosphere relaxed, particularly at the end of a night spent sampling the beer cellar!

### Restaurace Karolína★★
Karolíny Světlé, 14
☎ 24 23 54 52/06 28 88 500
Metro Národní třída
Open every day 11am-11pm.

This is a delightful place to eat in the summer months, with tables set out in the courtyard under the shade of the trees. The Czech cuisine is unpretentious and good value, and the service is friendly and attentive. It's a restful spot in a lovely setting.

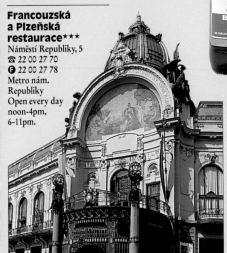

### U Dvou Koček★★

Uhelný trh, 10
☎ 24 22 99 82
Metro Můstek or Národní
třída
Open every day 11am-11pm.

This 17th-century tavern has become rather touristy, but it still manages to retain its warm, friendly atmosphere thanks to the accordion players who add a certain something to your meal (and your bill). The food is simple and excellent value.

### U Vejvodů★★

Jilská, 4
☎ 24 21 05 91
Metro Národní
třída
Open every day
10am-midnight.

The latest
Czech
establish-
ment to
offer local
cuisine and the
convivial atmosphere of a big tavern. A huge vat is suspended above the bar on the ground floor, where the beer flows freely. Expect to pay around Kč55 for the set meal, Kč80-130 à la carte.

### U Pavouka★★★

Celetná, 17
☎ 23 13 327
Metro nám. Republiky
Open every day 11am-midnight.

The restaurant is located in the huge medieval basement of the building, with its impressive arches and welcoming atmosphere. However, you do need to dress smartly here. The service is excellent, and you can enjoy tasty traditional Czech dishes. Try the halibut and the Bohemian-style roast duck. It's quite expensive but well worth the money.

## Nové Město

### Novoměstský pivovar★★

Vodičkova, 20
☎ 22 23 24 48
Metro Karlovo náměstí
Muzeum or Můstek
Open Mon.-Sat. 11am-11pm,
Sun. 10am-10pm.

This maze of beer halls has become very popular due to the excellent Czech food served here. On the menu is a delicious pork knuckle dish (*vepřové pečené koleno*), and the portions are very generous. To complement the tasty food try a glass of the beer, which is made on the premises. There's a friendly atmosphere, but prices have been raised due to its increased popularity. Always book ahead.

### Restaurace pivovarský dům★★★

Lípová, 511, Prague 2
☎ 96 21 66 66
Metro Karlovo náměstí
Open every day 11am-11.30pm.

Good, traditional Czech food served in a setting dedicated to the art of beer-making. The light beer is brewed in the basement of the building and is naturally cloudy and delicious. Ask for a tour of the brewery, which is very interesting. The dishes are very good value (Kč55-90) and the portions are generous. The location is also excellent and it is very difficult to make a choice between this restaurant and Novoměstský pivovar, so why not try them both!

### U Pinkasů★★

Jungmannovo nám, 15
Metro Můstek
☎ 24 23 08 28
Open every day 10am-10pm.
Although close to Wenceslas Square, this is still a regular haunt for the locals. Famed as the first *pivnice* to serve Pilsner Urquell, it continues to do so. It's on two floors and not immediately obvious from the outside. Enjoy the beer and goulash.

### U Rozvařilů★
Na Poříčí, 26
Metro nám. Republiky or Florenc
Open Mon.-Fri. 8am - 7.30pm, Sat. 9am-7pm, and Sun. 10am-5pm.

You can still find snack-bars in Prague (*bufet or samoobsluha*), and they serve excellent meals that are quick and good value. Take your pick from

sandwiches or hot dishes, and then decide whether to eat standing up, as regulars tend to, or at a table. If you're hungry and in a rush, this is an ideal spot and a favourite haunt of the locals.

### U Rumpálu★★★
Skoská 14, Prague 1
☎ 22 23 10 44
Metro Karlovo náměstí, Můstek or Muzeum.
Open Mon., Tue., Fri. 11am-11pm, Wed., Thu. 11am-midnight, Sat. 1pm-11pm, Sun. 5pm-11pm.

This basement restaurant has a French feel, with wooden tables and benches and pretty table-cloths. The food, however, is very Czech and includes some light dishes and a good salad bar.

### U Pravdů★★
Žitná, 15
☎ 22 23 19 29
Metro Karlovo náměstí, Můstek or Muzeum
Open every day 11am-11pm.

A regular haunt for locals, where there's always a warm welcome from the hospitable owner. The food is traditional Czech, with wholesome winter soups and some unusual dishes, including shark and kangaroo. On a sunny day you can eat in the garden.

### Skořepka★★
Skořepka, 1
☎ 24 21 47 15
Metro Můstek or Národní třída
Open every day 11am-midnight.

A pleasant, country-style inn decorated with wood, old tools and a real plough. The tasty local cuisine includes a number of traditional recipes. Set meal for around Kč55, à la carte Kč70-160.

### U Čížků ★★★
Karlovo nám, 34
☎ 22 23 22 57
Metro Karlovo náměstí
Open every day 10am-10pm.

Situated on Charles Square, this elaborately-decorated restaurant, with its velvet wall hangings and tapestry, serves traditional Czech food in large portions. Meat, game and fish are on the menu, and the food is tasty and quite light. *Plzeň* beer is served and booking is advisable.

## Vinohrady

### Rudý Baron★★
Korunní, 23
☎ 22 51 44 85
Metro nám. Miru
Open every day 11am-11.30pm.

The interior of this restaurant is dedicated to the pilots and planes of the First World War. You're guaranteed good meat dishes and a selection of well-cooked fish. If you present your pilot's licence you'll get a 10% discount.

### Vinárna U Jiříka★★
Vinohradská, 62
☎ 24 25 76 26
Metro Jiřího z Poděbrad
Open every day 11am-midnight.

This restaurant is well-located, and the food is very reasonably priced. Service can be slow, but the menu has a large selection of dishes, generous in size and attractively presented. Delicious starters will be brought to your table, but you should be aware that they'll be added to your bill.

# CAFÉS, TEA ROOMS AND CAKE SHOPS

## Malá Strana

### Kavárna Chimera
Lázeňská, 6
☎ 06 06 321 967
Trams 12, 22, Malostranské nám. stop
Open every day noon-midnight.

This art gallery/café is a favourite haunt of young people, with tables and chairs in different colours and comfortable sofas, and works of contemporary Czech artists on the walls. The atmosphere is warm and welcoming. You can have pastries, toast or more substantial snacks.

### V Karmelitské
Karmelitská, 20
☎ 90 05 80 67
Trams 12, 22, Malostranské nám. stop
Open Mon.-Fri. 7am-7pm, Sat. 10am-7pm, Sun. 10am-10pm.

The waiters are dressed in black trousers and white shirts in this café, which has a rather British feel to it. There's a large selection of pastries, Viennese breads and ice-creams. A pleasant and peaceful place to enjoy afternoon tea.

### Malostranská Kavárna
Malostranské nám., 5/28
☎ 53 94 34
Trams 12, 22, Malostranské nám. stop.

This is one of Prague's time-honoured cafés, founded in 1874 and recently renovated. Kafka was a regular visitor here. The three lovely vaulted rooms look out over Malostranská Square. Try the delicious pastries and iced coffee.

### U zeleného čaje
Nerudova, 19
☎ 57 53 00 27
Trams 12, 22, Malostranské nám. stop
Open every day 11am-10pm.

The 'Green Tea' is a great little café to stop at for refreshments in the heart of the tourist area. It has a lovely view onto Nerudova and a large selection of teas (green, black or herbal). There are also some home-made delicacies served on the local blue and white ceramic plates. It's a cosy place to go in winter.

## Staré Město

### Cafe Imperial
Nám. 14 října 16, Prague 5
☎ 27 78 04 25
Metro nám. Republiky
Open every day 11am-11pm.

Black and white-clad waiters weave their way between the columns of this strange café, which has an air of nostalgia about it. There are a few dishes available for around Kč90, with jazz concerts every Thursday, Friday and Saturday at 9pm.

### Café Divadlo na zábradlí
Aneňsk nám., 5
☎ 22 22 20 26
Metro Staroměstská
Open Mon.-Fri. 10am-1pm, and Sat.-Sun. 4pm-1am.

Located on the attractive Anenské Square, this café belongs to the famous Prague theatre. The mime artist Ladislav Fialka, a pupil of Marcel Marceau, and Václav Havel, then a stagehand, both came here. There are dedications to Czech actors on the walls and a small inner terrace. When you leave the café, take the little Stříbrná street with its uneven cobblestones and winding route.

### Café Konvikt
Bartolomějská, 11
☎ 24 23 24 27
Metro Národní třída
Open Mon.-Fri. 9am-1pm, Sat.-Sun. noon-1am.

This café is attached to the famous Czech cinema school, FAMU. There are black and white photos of international film celebrities on the walls. Take a seat in the room downstairs, overlooking a renovated courtyard. It has an arched ceiling and is very large and bright, which makes it a welcome relief from the usual smoky

atmosphere of other cafés. The furniture was salvaged from the 50s, which adds to the student feel of the place. You can also have snacks here.

## Kavárna Obecní Dům

Nám. Republiky, 5
☎ 22 00 21 11
Metro nám. Republiky
Open every day 7.30am-11pm.

The Municipal House café has an appropriately majestic Art

Nouveau interior. It's all crystal, chrome and mirrors, with waiters in uniform and piano music in the background. There's also a small booth (*salónek*) where you can access the Internet. You'll see elderly ladies and tourists looking somewhat overwhelmed, and it's a wonderful place to just sit and watch the world go by. Breakfast is served from 7.30-

11am, and main meals are served throughout the day.

## Týnská literární kavárna

Týnská, 6
Metro Můstek, Staroměstská or nám. Republiky
Open every day 10am-11pm.

This café is linked to the library next door and has a lovely terrace in a quiet courtyard. It's a stone's throw from the Old Town, just beside Týn courtyard (see p. 63), and has a selection of simple but tasty dishes.

## Odkolek

Rytířská, 12
Metro Můstek,
Open Mon.-Fri. 7am-8pm, Sat. 8am-8pm, Sun. 10am-8pm.

This is an ideal spot to enjoy traditional Czech pastries for breakfast. The decor is blue and white with natural wood. People start to queue at 7pm for the unsold cakes, which are then reduced by 30%. Order and pay at the counter before taking a seat.

(see p. 63)

## Nové Město

### Café Louvre

Národní třída, 20, 1st floor
☎ 29 76 65
Open every day 8am-11pm.

Once the haunt of a group of intellectuals, including Kafka and his friend Max Brod, this café was closed under the Communist regime and converted into offices. It has now been restored, and its doors are open once again. The waiters wear white aprons and bow ties, and the service is impeccable. Enjoy a coffee and cake while taking the opportunity to read the international papers.

### La Tonnelle wine bar

Anny Letenské 18, Prague 2
☎ 22 25 36 90
Ⓕ 22 25 44 45
Metro nám. Míru
Open Mon.-Fri, 3pm-midnight, Sat. 5pm-midnight

Prague's first French wine bar is set in the leafy Vinohrady district, once home to the royal vineyards. Wine is served by the glass (from Kč35) or by the bottle (from Kč210) with a plate of cheese or charcuterie.

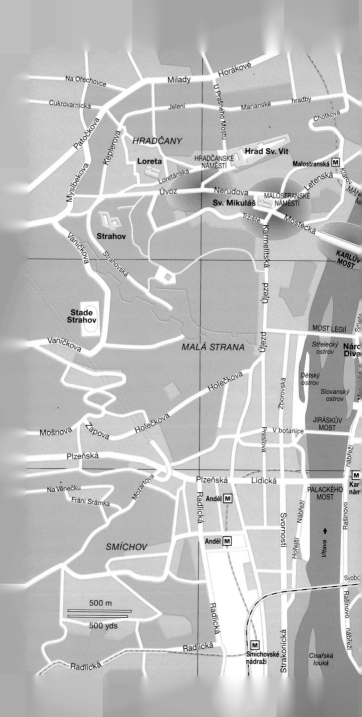

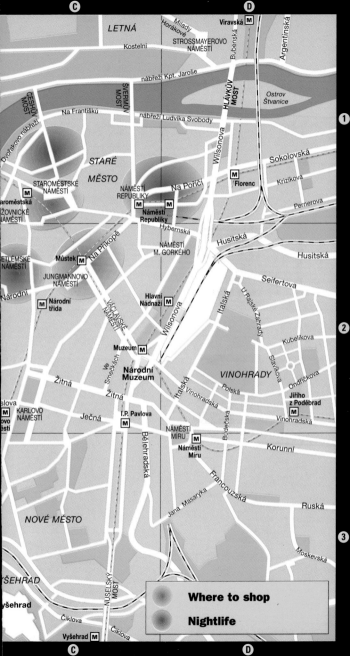

# shopping practicalities

Prague isn't yet a mecca for shoppers, but it's still possible to get some good bargains, particularly when buying local goods, including garnets, glass, crystal and wooden toys. Smoked meats and salamis are also good value, if you are looking for food bargains. You may well stumble upon some exciting and unusual objects in the antique shops or secondhand bookshops, as you walk around the city. Try to chat to the shop owners, and you'll get to know more about the real Prague.

Markets in Prague open early on weekdays but their closing times vary. You'll find that the shops are often very crowded on Saturdays and that it's easier to wander from shop to shop during the week, when there are noticeably fewer people about.

## OPENING HOURS

The smaller shops are usually open from 7-8am until 5-6pm, closing at 4pm on Fridays. Most of the larger stores are open Monday to Friday and until 1pm on Saturdays. However, there is a certain flexibility to these times, and you may find shops closed for no apparent reason during normal opening hours. The shops in the main centres are adapting their hours to the needs of the tourists, and they now remain open until at least 7pm, with no break for lunch.

## WHERE TO SHOP

You'll find souvenir and gift shops in the main tourist areas, including the route from the Old Town Square to the Castle, via Karlova and the Charles Bridge. Prices can vary dramatically from shop to shop. It's important to make a few comparisons before you actually buy anything. If you are looking for food or clothes, head for the lower end of Charles Square, around Národní třida, or in the area near the popular Tesco store.

Other good spots include Železná street and Celetna, near the Old Town Square.

### WHERE TO SHOP ON A SUNDAY

The best areas to head for on a Sunday include Charles Square, Na příkopě, Železná, Národní třida and the streets around the Old Town Square. The Little Quarter is a good spot for weekend shopping also. Most of the Czech shops and stores which sell foreign label goods are open on Saturdays and Sundays until 5pm.

## HOW TO BARGAIN

You'll usually find that goods have price tags attached, though this is frequently not the case in antique shops and secondhand bookshops. If an item has no price tag, then feel free to bargain. There are several methods, but the most simple and effective tactic is to ask the opening price, and then appear shocked. Gradually negotiate a more reasonable price, and you may find you're able to reduce the original by as much as 25%. Your success will depend upon your patience and acting ability!

## HOW TO PAY

Credit cards are gradually becoming more acceptable in Prague, but do check the stickers on the door of the shop, restaurant or hotel first. To be sure ask before you have your meal or commit yourself to a purchase. Your signature will be closely checked against your card, so take extra care when signing. If your card is lost or stolen, call the Prague credit card hotline on ☎ 23 66 688. It's a good idea to keep some cash for emergencies.

Do note that it's now illegal to pay in foreign currencies. You may be asked if you have American Dollars, German Marks or Pounds Sterling, but you must refuse.

## SALES AND BARGAINS

Sales (*sleva*) are becoming more popular with the arrival of Western stores. Clothes, shoes and

accessories are often sold off at good reductions (up to 50% from the end of August until September or October). Some sales start after New Year, and the best places to try are around Old Town Square, Wenceslas Square, Na příkopě and ul. 28. října.

Food is generally much cheaper than in the West, but other goods are gradually becoming more expensive as multi-nationals establish themselves in the city. The range of goods is increasing steadily.

## CUSTOMS REGULATIONS

Exporting antiques can be a laborious affair and you will have to pay 20% duty, as well as obtaining authorisation from the:
**Museum of Decorative Arts** (Uměleckoprůmyslové) Ul. 17. listopadu 2, Prague 1 ☎ 51 09 31 11 (For more information see p. 7.)

In any case, you'll find that antiques or *objets d'art* more than one hundred years old are rare and very difficult to come by.

FINDING YOUR WAY AROUND

In the Shopping and Nightlife sections, you'll find a reference after each address to its position on the map on p. 78-79.

## SHIPPING GOODS HOME

If you buy a heavy item, such as a piece of furniture, which is less than 30 years old, you can arrange for it to be transported home. The price is generally fixed and is based on volume. You'll need a photocopy of your passport, a photocopy of the invoice, a document confirming that you're a tourist in Prague, a certificate from the shop and a document showing the list of your purchases and the total amount paid. You should always keep the invoice. You may be asked to show it at customs, and you'll find it useful if you decide to sell your item in the future. It will also be needed for insurance purposes in the event of theft.

Contact **AGS Prague** to arrange transport worldwide. Klicany, 67, 250 69 Vodochody. ☎ 26 85 78 41 🅕 26 85 72 16.

## WOMEN'S FASHION

Fashion in Central Europe still has some way to go before it can compete with the West, but things are changing. Some designers are moving away from heavy cloth and sombre colours and introducing clothes with a lighter, brighter feel. Watch this space – Prague may be the next Paris or Milan. Here's a selection of some of the most interesting shops to visit. See page 125 for details of sizes.

### Galerie Módy - Lucerna

Štěpánská, 61 (C2)
☎ 24 21 15 14
Mon.-Sat. 10am-8pm.

This very elegant store, located in the Lucerna Palace, is an ideal showcase for new Czech collections. The work of over 20 designers is on show on the first floor, where you'll get a good idea of all the latest trends. The designers use mostly natural materials, with linen a popular cloth, and the colours are generally dark, with an emphasis on brown and black. You should be able to buy a little black evening dress for Kč2,000-2,500 and a pair of smart trousers will cost around Kč3,990. Before you leave, stop for a drink in the lovely little Café Galeria, located in the same building, where you can review your purchases in the ideal spot to appreciate the magnificent Art Nouveau architecture of the Lucerna Palace (see p. 55).

### Piano Boutique

Národní, 37 (C2)
☎ 24 21 32 82
(and Vinohradská, 47)

The clothes in this shop are very subtle in style and colour, but with an extra touch of Czech imagination. There are lovely dresses (Kč3,500), lightweight

knitted jumpers by Hana Marková (Kč1,200) and a range of beautiful leather handbags in many different sizes by Marcela Kotěšovcová (from Kč3,000-4,000).

### Modes Robes

Benediktská, 5 (C1)
☎ 24 82 60 16
Open Mon.-Fri. 10am-7pm, Sat. 10am-4pm.

♣ R ♠ S ♠
M O D E S
♦ B ♥ B ♦
S E D O M
♠ S ♦ R ♣

**MODES ROBES**

ODĚVY A DOPLŇKY, MINIGALERIE
BENEDIKTSKÁ 5
110 00 PRAHA 1
tel.: (4202)2322461

With the dresses crumpled and crammed onto the racks, you may not be too impressed by this collection at first. It's worth having a good look, however, as you may come across some interesting fabrics, even if the cut isn't impressive. Prices range from Kč1,200-1,600

### Black Market

Petrské nám (C1)
☎ 23 17 033
Open Mon.-Fri. noon-7pm, Sat. 10am-6pm.

This shop has a large selection of designer seconds – have a good hunt round to find the hidden treasures. You'll find sunglasses from Kč90 and feather boas at around Kč590. Nylon dresses and trousers start at Kč590.

## Devata Vina

Saská ulice (B1)
☎ 21 29 41 71
Open every day 11am-7pm.

At last some bright colours! Red, yellow, orange, plastic handbags, synthetic fabrics – the selection is amazing. Even if you're just popping in for a pair of tights (Kč400), you'll come out feeling brighter, although you may wish you'd worn your sunglasses.

## Klára Nademlýnská

Dlouhá, 7 (C1)
☎ 24 81 87 69
Open Mon.-Fri. 10am-7pm,
Sat. noon-6pm.

Undoubtedly Prague's top designer, Klára trained in Paris and has created a range of simple yet sophisticated suits, dresses and separates. Beautifully cut and made of high quality fabric, they are very reasonably priced.

## Delmas

Vodičková, 36 (C2)
☎ 24 23 91 32
Open Mon.-Fri. 9am-7pm,
Sat. 10am-5pm.

This is *the* place for handbags. You'll find a large selection of Czech bags, mostly inspired by Italian designers. Depending on the season, the colours can be bright (yellow, blue and orange) or more

## HATS – A PRAGUE TRADITION AND SPECIALITY

The hatmaking tradition is still very strong in Prague and there's a hat for every occasion — hats for evening wear and hats for day wear, hats to keep you warm and hats to keep you cool. You'll find a huge range of women's hats in classic styles, as well as in more unusual shapes and colours, made of felt (from Kč1,500) or natural straw (from Kč800).

A good place to shop for hats is Model Praha Družstvo, Wenceslas Square, 28 (C2), ☎ 24 21 68 05. It's open Mon.-Fri. 9am-7pm and Sat. 10am-5pm. The staff are very friendly and helpful, and you can ask their advice — they're happy to talk hats all day, as long as they come from this shop.

restrained (brown and black). With classic or more original styles, all of excellent quality, the prices are reasonable and you'll be impressed with the range and finish of the bags.

# MEN'S FASHION

It must be said that Prague isn't the place to come to overhaul your wardrobe, but you can find some interesting accessories, including belts and ties. If you're feeling nostalgic for the style of the 70s, then this is the place for you. There's a wide selection of new and secondhand clothing from the era, all at affordable prices. Indulge your passion for your favourite fashion – bell bottoms and kipper ties galore await you. See page 125 for details of sizes.

### Karpet
Nerudova, 18 (B1)
☎ 53 39 823
Open every day 8am-8pm.

If you're walking up towards the Castle on Nerudova Street (see p. 48), you won't be able to resist popping into this lovely shop which, despite its name, actually sells hats. Whether you're looking for felt or straw, peaked cap or boater, you won't be disappointed. Prices range from Kč200-650. You can also just enjoy browsing through the huge range of hats on display.

### O.P. Prostějof
Vodičkova 33, Prague 1 (C2)
☎ 21 61 51 52
Open Mon.-Fri. 9am-7pm, Sat. 10am-6pm.

The defining name in Czech men's ready-to-wear, this old establishment is very popular for its two- and three-piece suits. Made of flannel, wool and cotton, they come in dark colours, including black, navy and dark grey, and cost Kč6,000-9,000. There are also some Czech-made ties (Kč200).

### Los Hadros
Víta Nejedlého 3, Prague 3 (not on map)
☎ 22 71 32 52
Open Mon.-Fri. 11am-8pm.

Los Hadros means 'tea cloths' in Czech-Spanish, which may explain why the shop sells a variety of colourful secondhand clothes. You'll find 1970s-style cotton and synthetic men's shirts with spots or flowers that can be teamed with red or green trousers. There are women's secondhand clothes too.

### King Charles

Dlouhá tr., 31 (C1)
☎ 23 10 560
Open Mon.-Thu. 10am-7pm.

This shop is for smokers only. Everything in it is dedicated to the love of tobacco and pipe-smoking. Connoisseurs can choose from a wide selection of wooden pipes (from around Kč120), and then fill them with local tobacco, available in packets or metal boxes.

### Dům Módy

Wenceslas Square, 58 (C2)
☎ 96 15 81 11
Open Mon.-Fri. 9am-8pm, Sat. 9am-4pm.

You won't be able to transform your wardrobe in this shop, which focuses very much on local fashion. Don't expect to find good suit bargains either, but do have a look through the shirt section, where you'll come across the Janek label. This Czech designer makes beautiful classic cotton shirts

(from Kč800-1,300). Alternatively, why not treat yourself to a pair of flannelette pyjamas (from Kč600), which are warm and comfortable if not quite at the cutting edge of fashion.

### Bat'a

Wenceslas Square, 6 (C2)
☎ 24 21 81 33

Open Mon.-Fri. 9am-9pm, Sat. 9am-6pm, Sun. 10am-6pm.

This famous establishment (see p. 53), is known world-wide and is the place to come if you're looking for men's footwear. There's an entire floor devoted to sports shoes, another to walking shoes, and the third and final floor has formal shoes, both by Bat'a and other shoe manufacturers. Even if you don't want to buy any shoes, you can still enjoy the magnificent view over Wenceslas Square from the top floor. Bat'a also stocks women's and children's shoes.

### Delmas

Vodičkova 36, Prague 1 (C2)
☎ 96 23 69 23
Open Mon.-Fri. 9am-7pm, Sat. 10am-5pm.

A leather shop specialising in a fine range of Czech-made leather goods. The designs are traditional but the articles are well made and beautifully finished. They include a large range of brown and black briefcases (around Kč4,000), notepad holders (Kč2,500), wallets (Kč985) and belts.

see p. 53

### 'A ROSE BY ANY OTHER NAME'

You may be surprised to discover so many young women walking around with a flower in their hand and a man on their arm. It's a very strong Czech tradition to buy a flower, preferably a rose, for your partner for the evening. Even if you take your date to the best restaurant in Prague, she won't be impressed if you don't turn up with a rose. Roses are available at the many flower stalls in the city, so there's no excuse if you turn up without one.

These make ideal gifts for the man in your life. You'll even find a few walking sticks (Kč900) tucked away at the back of the shop.

# CHILDREN'S TOYS AND CLOTHES

Prague is a wonderful place to buy traditional toys for children. Hand-carved toys and wooden puppets will continue to delight children long after the latest electronic gadget has been tossed aside. It's an opportunity to fill up your Santa sack in readiness for Christmas!

### Art Dekor
Adria Palace,
Národní třída, 40 (C2)
☎ 24 49 46 30
Open Mon.-Fri. 10am-6pm,
Sat.-Sun. 10am-4pm.

The extraordinary combination of the Art Nouveau gallery and nearby Rondo-Cubist palace

(from Kč293) and other amusing wooden toys, painted in lovely bright colours. Games and soft toys are also on sale. You'll find something to delight every child, or you might just end up keeping the purchase for yourself.

may have inspired the designer of the imaginative fabric toys on sale here. There are elephants with polka dots, rabbits with stripes, rhinos with flowers and many more unusual creatures. They're all hand-made originals and prices range from Kč150-400. Buy a child's quilted bedspread to match the toy or choose a contrasting fun fabric.

### Hračky Kid-Trnka
Ostrovní, 21 (C2)
☎ 29 67 53
Open Mon.-Fri. 10.30am-7pm, Sat. 11am-4pm.

This shop's yellow frontage bears the name of the famous Czech puppet maker. Inside, there are delightful wooden puppets

### Krokodil
Bartolomějská, 3 (C2)
☎ 24 22 81 01
Open Mon.-Fri. 10am-6pm,
Sat.-Sun. 9am-noon.

The name Krokodil is a bit of a red herring, since the shops sells electric trains and accessories. You can buy Czech brands, including Zerba (Kč530-850) and Vacek (Kč650 for a Budweiser carriage), as well as foreign makes, such as the impressive Austrian Rocco trains (Kč850-3,000). You'll also find a range of accessories and figures, with which to decorate your network.

### Pecka – Modelář

Karoliny Světlé, 3 (B2)
☎ 23 23 445
☎ 24 23 01 70
Zlanická, 4 (C1)
☎ 23 23 445
☎ 23 29 079
**Open Mon.-Fri.
10am-6pm,
Sat. 9am-noon.**

Model enthusiasts will be excited to find rare Czech pieces at excellent prices in this shop, which has two branches. You can buy a kit of

the Škoda Favorit, the popular Czech car, costing Kč72 for the 96 rally version. If you'd prefer to make a model plane, they're also available here. Try to take advantage of the sales, when prices can be very attractive.

### Modely

Havelská, 10 (C2)
☎ 24 23 01 70
**Open Mon.-Fri. 9am-6pm,
Sat. 9am-4pm.**

This is a miniature paradise. The window display has cars of all makes and materials, with the metal ones carefully lined up as if a race is about to start. Model enthusiasts can learn all there is to know in this store, and have a good chance of getting an original. The Tatra shown below cost Kč2,200.

### Galerie U Zravýho Kocoura

Palackého 11, Prague 1 (C2)
☎ 24 94 73 81
**Open Mon.-Fri. 10am-6pm,
Sat. 10am-3pm.**

The brightly-coloured naïve paintings on sale here are very decorative, and some are already framed. There are also drawings, reproductions and paintings on glass, ideal for children's bedroom walls. They come in a variety of subjects (from Noah's Ark to farm animals) and a range of prices (from Kč400 to 5,000).

### Prodejna

Karlova, 23 (C1)
☎ 26 18 82
**Open Mon.-Sat. 10am-6pm.**

Almost lost in the heart of Karlova with all its tourist attractions, this shop has an enormous selection of toys, all made in the Czech Republic. You can buy small traditional characters (from Kč200-400) or a small crib complete with animals. Larger items include a miniature dining room made of natural or painted wood (Kč1,350). This shop is a real find – make sure you don't miss it if you're looking for lovely gifts that are made locally.

### Balet

Karolíny Světlé, 22 (B2)
☎ 22 22 10 63
**Open Mon.-Fri. 10am-6pm.**

In this old shop, situated close to the Vltava river, tutus hang from the ceiling, and ballet shoes, pink tights and leotards galore await excited little ballet pupils. Ballet shoes cost from Kč379 and leotard prices start at around Kč400. An atmosphere steeped in classical dance, this shop is bound to impress children interested in ballet.

### THE STORY OF MIKULÁŠ, A DEVIL AND AN ANGEL

On 5 December, Mikuláš (St Nicholas) looks for children in the streets of Prague. Accompanied by a devil in red and an angel, he distributes treats to the well-behaved children. As night falls, the little citizens of Prague watch his carriage go past and hear the gifts being given out. Those who have misbehaved and are unable to recite a poem receive potatoes and coal instead of sweets.

# MUSICAL INSTRUMENTS AND RECORDINGS

The Czech musical tradition goes back to the Middle Ages and the country has an excellent reputation for the quality of its musical instruments. Brass instruments made here are very reasonable. If you need to assemble an entire brass band, you'll be able to do it much more cheaply in Prague than in many other cities. Good secondhand bargains are around, but try not to fall under the spell of an antique Bohemian violin, which could seriously upset your finances.

### Amati – Denak
U Obecního domu (C1)
☎ 22 00 23 46
Open Mon.-Fri. 10am-6pm.

This shop is next to the Municipal House and specialises in brass

instruments from the Amati Kraslice workshops. Towards 1550, the first instrument makers set themselves up in the old mining town of Kraslice, a tradition which continued for more than four hundred years. Clarinets, saxophones, trumpets, oboes, French horns and other instruments are sold here, including the piccolo trumpet (see also Martin Kukla – Blues).

### Guitar Parc
Jungmannovo nám., 17 (C2)
☎ 24 22 25 00
Open Mon.-Fri. 9am-7pm, Sat. 9am-3pm.

The flutes alone are worth coming for, but you'll also find string, wind and percussion instruments, as well as guitars and pianos. Or you could even just look through the range of music scores if you like. The entrance can be found on the first floor.

### Martin Kukla – Blues
Lucerna Passage
Štěpánská, 61 (C2)
☎ 24 21 70 77
Open Mon.-Fri. 10am-7pm.

The piccolo trumpet is made in the Czech Republic and is the smallest trumpet in the world. It looks at first just like a beautiful chrome toy, but once you hear some Baroque music being played on it, you realise it is far from being a mere plaything. Martin Kukla sells them for around Kč5,600, and you'll find them next to a range of acoustic and electric guitars, not far from the saxophones, both new and secondhand.

### Talacko
Rybná, 29
☎ 23 26 302
✆ 23 26 310
talacko@mbox.vol.cz

Established by a Czech-Australian composer, Talacko is a mine of sheet music, with a selection ranging from popular to classic.

## COMPLETE YOUR COLLECTION

Classical CDs are generally good value in Prague, though the choice can be a bit limited. Contrary to what you may have heard, the recording quality is often excellent. It's a good opportunity for classical buffs to expand their collections at very attractive prices. Here are some suggestions of places to try, where you should find a good selection.

**Supraphon** (classical)
☎ 24 94 87 19
Jungmannova, 20 (C2)
Open Mon.-Fri. 9am-7pm,
Sat. 9am-1pm.
**Popron Megastore** (classical in the basement, and rock)
☎ 24 94 86 76
Jungmannova, 30 (C2).
Open Mon.-Fri. 9am-8pm,
Sat, 9am-7pm, Sun. 9am-6pm.

## Capriccio
Újezd, 15 (B2)
☎ and 📠 53 25 07
Open Mon.-Fri. 9am-6pm,
Sat. 10am-2pm.

You'll find hundreds of music scores for a whole range of instruments at this shop. There are pieces for beginners, as well as classical music and pop music, with a strong emphasis on jazz. Musicians will love it here, and CDs are on sale as well.

## Hudební nástroje Jakub Lis
Náprstkova, 10 (C2)
☎ 22 22 11 10
Open Mon.-Fri. 10am-7pm,
Sat.-Sun. 10am-5pm.

You may be surprised to discover how much Czechs adore American country music, and it isn't just in response to the latest musical in town. It runs much deeper, as revealed by the cowboy jackets, saloon-style bars and Czech translations of song lyrics which you may encounter on your travels. In this shop you can buy and sell secondhand and antique instruments on which to play your favourite folk and country music. You'll find a selection of concert programmes next to the CDs.

## U Sv. Martina
Martinská, 4 (C2)
☎ and 📠 26 65 15
Open Mon.-Fri. 10am-1pm,
2-6pm, Sat. 10am-7pm.

You'll get a warm welcome from this specialist in Bohemian instruments, new and secondhand, and he'll be more than happy to share with you his expertise in violins and accordions. Several of the violins in the shop may have already been sold, but do ask about any instrument that catches your eye. Even if it isn't for sale, you can find out where to get one like it.

# JEWELLERY AND CRYSTAL

Gems, precious stones, silver and pearls are all available in Prague. You can choose from genuine or costume jewellery, real or imitation, chic or kitsch. Don't forget to buy a set of crystal glasses to brighten up your table at home. They make an excellent conversation point.

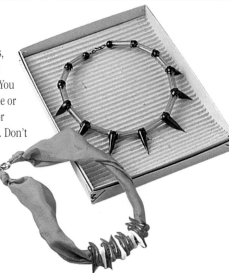

### Halada
Karlova,
25 (C2)
☎ 24 23 89 28
Open every day 9am-7pm.

Before you reach Charles Bridge, drop in at this shop and discover some of Prague's most beautiful silver jewellery. There are stunning earrings (from Kč1,300), simple or elaborate rings (Kč400-1,700) and a selection of pendants (from Kč2,000), in matt or polished silver, plain or set with stones. You'll be simply spoilt for choice.

### Nikkita & Inkognito
Vodičkova, 20 (C2)
☎ 06 02 613 481
Mon.-Fri. 11am-7pm.

The colourful beads of the Inkognito collection of necklaces shimmer on their metal threads (from Kč190). There are also some attractive one-off skirts (Kč1,500) and dresses (Kč2,000-3,000) bearing the successful Nikkita label. The entrance to the shop is in Novoměstská Passage.

### East Art Gallery
Wenceslas Square, 23 (C2)
Open every day 10am-8pm.

Great magical powers have been attributed to amber, and it's thought to be a fertility symbol and healing stone. Many jewellers in Prague work with yellow amber, which comes mostly from the Baltic region. However, be careful of the many imitations. You can check the quality by rubbing pieces of amber together and then sniffing them. You'll notice that it gives off a distinct smell if it's the real thing. In this gallery you'll come across some lovely amber pieces, and prices start from Kč2,000-4,000 for a large necklace.

## Stříbrné Sperky

Wenceslas Square, 19 (C2)
☎ 24 21 36 27

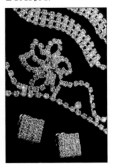

Open every day 10am-7pm,
Sun. 10am-6pm.

In this jewellery shop you'll discover imitation cultured pearls, glass beads of every imaginable colour, sparkling earrings and brilliant pendants. It's a wonderful place to buy jewellery to get you noticed. A necklace will cost from Kč200.

## Holman Shop

Malé nám., 4 (C1)
☎ 24 21 27 19
Open every day 10am-7pm.

Up on the first floor, you'll find a wide range of crystal, pearl and diamanté jewellery at very reasonable prices, as well as hair slides and some Czech glass. You will also find a selection of ladies' evening wear as well as high fashion items.

## Granát Turnov

Dlouhá, 28-30 (C1)
☎ 23 15 612
Open Mon.-Wed. 10am-5pm,
Sat. 10am-1pm.

This shop has a large selection of garnets, set in gold, silver and platinum, which come directly from a craftsman's cooperative in Turnov. The pieces are original and sold at factory outlet prices. A silver or platinum garnet ring will cost from Kč1,500. If set in gold, a ring will cost from Kč2,700.

## Crystalex

Malé nám., 6 (C1)
☎ 24 22 84 59
Open every day 10am-8pm.

Head for the Malá Strana along Melantrichova street, where you'll pass several shops selling crystal. The shop windows are

overflowing with glasses and decanters. At this Crystalex outlet you'll be able to buy a selection of pieces at reasonable prices, possibly the best in Prague. A set of six glasses will cost from Kč1,800. A decanter with a coloured glass stopper will set you back around Kč455. The design of the pieces is mostly classic,

cut, engraved and coloured. If you need to buy a very special gift then this is the place to come.

## Detail

Melantrichova, 11 (C2)
☎ 24 21 05 94
Open Mon.-Fri. 10am-6pm.

The five Detail shops in Prague sell only silver jewellery in stylised modern designs. They're sometimes set with semi-precious stones, and include pendants, necklaces, brooches and pretty matt silver rings for around Kč1,000. Look out for the garnets, which blend perfectly with the modern jewellery.

## STATIONERY

In this hi-tech age of emails and the internet, old-fashioned stationery still has a certain charm. If you still use pens and paper, you'll love looking round the stationery shops in Prague, where the products are amazing value. The notebooks and journals come in all shapes and sizes, from kitsch to Art Deco. Some stock is available on recycled paper, so you can be eco-friendly if you wish. Artists can also stock up on paper and materials here at very reasonable prices.

### Papírnictví

Mikulandská, 7 (C2)
☎ 90 05 50 76
Open Mon.-Fri. 9am-6pm.
Papírnictví, Miroslav Zunt
Malostranské nám., 27
Open Mon.-Fri. 8.30am-6pm, Sat. 9am-1pm.

There's a nostalgic atmosphere in these two stationers'. The choice is more limited than in the supermarkets, but shopping in the old-fashioned and slightly dusty atmosphere of these small shops is much more enjoyable.

### Tesco

Národní třída, 26 (C2)
☎ 22 00 31 11
Open Mon.-Fri. 8am-8pm, Sat. 9am-6pm, Sun. 10am-6pm.

Make sure you see the huge range of locally produced paper on the second floor. There is also a traditional selection of notebooks and journals, some using recycled paper, modelling clay, colouring books and pens of all shapes and sizes. Head for the wrapping paper section, which is full of good ideas. Decorate your gift with printed or gilded paper (Kč17-27), gift boxes (Kč6-14) and paper bows in all colours (Kč10).

### Mc Paper & Co

Dukelských hrdinů, 39
☎ 33 38 00 02
Trams 12, 7,
Štrossmayerovo nám. stop
Open Mon.-Fri. 8.30am-6.30pm, Sat. 9am-noon.

It's self-service at this shop. You have to take a basket with you as you browse, but you can take as much time as you like making your selection. You'll find the range is the same

as at Tesco, but the prices are fractionally cheaper. Enjoy a good rummage here.

### Object Gift Shop

U lužického semináře, 19 (B1)
☎ 57 31 80 56
Open every day 10am-8pm.

This shop isn't officially a stationer's, but it sells all sorts of paper and cardboard products. The selection includes puppets to make yourself (Kč60), colourful notebooks, lovely frames (Kč125-170), and photo albums covered in bright fabrics (Kč175-370).

### Museum of Decorative Arts shop

17 Listopadu, 2 (C1)
☎ 24 37 32 64
Open every day exc. Mon. 10am-6pm.

In this tiny shop, tucked away under the steps leading to the

museum itself, you'll come across notebooks and good quality exercise books. Some have Art Deco covers (see above) and you can buy large format notepads, with recycled paper, for your photos or postcards of Prague. Before you leave, climb the steps to the toilets to see the unique view over the Jewish cemetery from an unusual vantage point.

creations, people fly over Charles Bridge and the Golem wanders the streets. Nothing escapes his touch, he has even created designs for Prague's beer. Beware the price of his pieces – some shops are unscrupulous about inflating them.

### Zlatá Loď
Náprstkova, 4 (C2)
☎ 22 22 01 74
🖷 260 855
Open Mon.-Fri. 9.30am-6pm, Sat. 10am-5pm.

### Cartes Unicef
Národní, 20 (C2)
☎ 24 48 45 51
Open Tue.-Wed. 1-5pm.

Unicef cards offer an alternative to Czech humour and taste. Choose your cards from the selection in the shop window on the street, and make your way down the narrow corridor to the counter to be served.

### Design Fun Explosiv
Perlová, 1 (C2)
☎ 21 66 72 59
Open every day 10am-6pm.

You'll find Jiří Votruba's designs everywhere in Prague. His illustrations adorn a whole range of souvenirs, from T-shirts to table mats. Since 1990, he has been trying to 'show the public the history and culture of Prague in a non-traditional way'. In his imaginative

This is a good place to buy art materials at extremely reasonable prices. It also offers an excellent opportunity to test some locally made products (Kč269 for 48 pastels, Kč789 for a wooden box containing 24 watercolours).

### Altamira
Jilská, 2 (C2)
☎ 24 21 99 50
Open Mon.-Fri. 9am-7pm, Sat. 10am-5pm.

You can hardly put one foot in front of the other in this shop. The articles are piled on top of one another

## ALL THE COLOURS OF THE RAINBOW

Koh-i-Noor has nothing to do with the famous diamond, but it's certainly a gem of a brand. It has an excellent range of pencils at good prices, made in České Budějovice. Individual lead pencils cost Kč3, a wooden box of ten costs Kč127 and you'll pay from Kč135 for coloured pencils. Children will love the large container in the shape of a coloured pencil, full of crayons (Kč29 for 12 and Kč427 for the full container). The brand is available in most stationery shops in Prague.

apparently at random. Customers aren't allowed to touch anything and have to wait to be served. You'll find all the basic artist's materials for oil painting, water colours, modelling and sculpture on sale here, so come and stock up.

# DEPARTMENT STORES AND MARKETS

Shopping in the department stores of Prague can be an interesting experience, particularly in the food sections, where the selection is usually the most extensive in the store. You should also visit the traditional markets, where you can buy everything from fresh fruit to furniture and from caviar to crockery. They offer a more practical and often cheaper alternative.

## DEPARTMENT STORES

### Tesco

Národní třída, 26 (C2)
☎ 22 00 31 11
Mon.-Fri. 7am-8pm, Sat. 9am-6pm, Sun. 10am-6pm.

Originally known as Máj, this store was sold to K-Mart who then sold it on to Tesco in 1996. You'll find nearly everything imaginable and British expatriates shop here because of the choice and quality in the food department located in the basement. There are local products, together with imported Western goods, and also an excellent bakery with Czech and French bread. Prices are slightly higher than most places but they're worth paying for the variety. Have a quick look at the leather bags (Kč1,500-3,000) and straw hats (Kč100) on the ground floor.

The stationery department is worth a visit (see p. 92), and the hi-fi department on the fourth floor has a large selection of blank cassettes at good prices.

### Kotva

Nám. Repuliky, 8 (C1)
☎ 24 80 11 11
Open Mon.-Fri. 9am-8pm,
Sat. 9am-6pm,
Sun. 10am-6pm.

Built in the 60s, Kotva was once one of the most important shopping centres in Central Europe. Today, however, with the exception of the food department in the basement, it has an old-fashioned and rather dull look. It's worth taking a tour of all the floors (crockery, clothes, books etc.), and while you're here take advantage of this rather curious establishment by replenishing your stock of hair accessories at cheap prices (from Kč15-50).

### Krone

Václavské nám. 21,
Prague 1 (C2)
Open Mon.-Fri. 8am-7pm,
Sat. 8am-6pm, Sun.
10am-6pm.

This store stands half-way along
the great Václavské Avenue.
The floors devoted to men's,
women's and children's fashion
are of little interest, but you'll
also find a small stationery
department and some reasonably-
priced costume jewellery on the
ground floor, as well as a food
section in the basement where
you can buy Czech specialities
(charcuterie, spirits, etc.).

## LOCAL MARKETS

### Havel Market

(Known as
Havelský trh)
Havelská (C2)
Open Mon.-Fri.
8am-6pm,
Sat. 9am-1pm.

In this open-air
market, with its
huge selection of
vegetables, cut
flowers and pots
of honey, you'll find
craft items, such as
painted eggs
(Kč150-300),
postcards and
prints. There's a
friendly, relaxed
atmosphere, so
take time to wander

around and hunt out little
wooden gifts or pendants set
with stones (from Kč50).

### Správa Tržiště

Národní třída,
near metro (C2)
Open Mon.-Fri.
9am-5pm,
Sat.-Sun. 9am-4pm.

At the exit to Tesco (see p.
94), there's a fruit and
vegetable market. The
produce is good value, but the
quality can vary, depending on
the season. You can buy dried

fruits, almonds, chocolate-
covered nuts, and dried bananas
in locally-made yoghurt. It's a

good place to stock up on
nourishing food on a chilly day.

## SEASONAL MARKETS

At Christmas and Easter, market
stalls are set up on the Old
Town Square and at the
lower end of Wenceslas
Square. The locals
come to keep
warm with a
glass of

mulled
wine, while
tourists walk
round the stalls, tempted by the
smell of grilled sausages with
bread and mustard (párek).
Painted eggs, beeswax candles
and straw decorations are on sale
at Christmas, along with other
crafts. It's quite a festive event.

## LOCAL CRAFTS

Wooden objects, puppets, crystal and traditional blue tablecloths are probably the most common examples of Czech craft, but you'll also find there is a wide range of good-quality, reasonably-priced small gifts to take home. If you come to the city in December, you can also look out for Christmas decorations – which will add a hint of Bohemia to your usual festive decor.

### Beruška
Pasáž Černá Růže,
Na Příkopě, 12 (C2)
☎ 21 01 46 07
Open Mon.-Fri. 9am-8pm,
Sat. 9am-7pm,
Sun. 11am-7pm.

Beruška ('the ladybird') sells brightly-coloured painted wooden objects for children, including large

quantities of toys (from little trains to cute frogs), pretty mobiles (bees gathering pollen for Kč250) and other naïve decorative objects for children's rooms.

### Obchod U sv. Jilji
Jilská, 7 (C2)
☎ 24 23 26 95
Open every day 10am-7pm.

Handmade puppets, in wood or plaster, inspired by traditional antique models, are on sale in this shop in the heart of old Prague. You could buy an entire troupe and stage a show when

you get back home. For the less ambitious, prices for a single puppet start at Kč480.

### Lidová jizba
Wenceslas Square, 14 (C2)
Open every day 10am-6pm.

Far from the noise of Wenceslas Square and hidden at the end of a narrow alley, this shop will give you the warmest welcome. Take your time to choose a tablecloth, either with the traditional blue motifs or with stripes (from around Kč420). Plan your next Christmas colour scheme, Czech-style this time, using only red decorations.

### Móda Original
Jungmannova, 13 (C2)
☎ 96 24 50 33
Open Mon.-Fri. 10am-6pm.

From the blue ceramics with their stylised motifs, beeswax candles and stationery to the tablecloths, table mats and linen dresses and blouses, everything in this shop is handmade in the Czech Republic. With their simple lines and subtle colours (China blue and soft green), the clothes are both elegant and attractive.

### Max-Loyd
Ovocný trh, 12 (C2)
☎ 21 63 71 80
Open every day 10am-7pm.

A small craft shop where fine plain blue ceramic tea sets sit side by side with mugs decorated with colourful designs, painted metal containers of every size (much prized in Prague), tablecloths and table mats made of homespun fabric, original hand-made glasses and an assortment of aromatic and herbal teas.

### Atelier Kavka

Dlouhá, 44 (C1)
☎ 24 82 82 49
Open Mon.-Fri. 10am-7pm, Sat. 10am-4pm.

With its abundance of floral arrangements, decorative items and old furniture, this shop is like a little perfumed green haven. A bouquet of dried flowers costs from Kč2,500. There are also large glass and metal dishes (from Kč1,200), small vases (Kč390) and ceramic plates (Kč690 for a set).

### Lobeli

Újezd, 16 (B2)
☎ 53 05 02
Elišky Krásnohorské, 1 (C1)
☎ 23 20 734
Open Mon.-Fri. 10am-7pm, Sat. 10am-5pm.

If you're keen on antique furniture but don't like restoring it, then this is the place for you. There are two shops brimming with old wooden Czech furniture, cleaned, renovated and waxed. There's a huge selection of items,

all ready to go, including chests of drawers, wardrobes, dressers, chairs and tables. The prices are attractive too, starting at around Kč3,000-15,000. They will be happy to give you information about about transporting goods home. (See p. 81.)

### Atelier trnka

Újezd, 46 (B2)
☎ 90 00 09 75
Open Mon.-Fri. 9am-6pm, Sat. 9am-1pm.

If you want to give your sofa a new look, change your cushions, or update your curtains or quilt, you can choose from one of the many locally made fabrics in this unpretentious haberdasher's shop. There are warm-coloured fabrics with stripes and thick upholstery fabrics to choose from, along with a lighter cotton range. You won't find much in

### ČESKÁ LIDOVÁ REMESLA

You'll recognise this chain from its shop windows, which are always full to the brim with

wooden objects and blue printed fabric. All the natural products give the stores a warm and inviting atmosphere. You can buy embroidered tablecloths (Kč635), wicker baskets (Kč375), painted eggs (Kč50-180), pure wool jumpers (Kč4,500), kitchen equipment (Kč15-90) and small decorative items. You should visit one of their eight stores to see the best of traditional Czech crafts. Try the one at Melantrichova, 17 (C2). Open Mon.-Fri. 10am-7pm, Sat.-Sun. 10am-7.30pm.

the way of plain or floral material, but there's plenty to tempt you to change your colour scheme back home. There's a wide selection of cloth, all made in the Czech Republic, and the prices are very reasonable. It's a great place to come if you need some inspiration for your tired-looking furnishings.

## SPORT

Although the Czechs have produced such wonderful tennis players as Jana Novotná, Petr Korda, Ivan Lendl and the great Martina Návratilová, the national sport is, ice hockey, and children can be seen skating on the smallest pond in winter. The Czechs are extremely proud of their national team, which beat the USSR in August 1968, Canada in 1996 and became Olympic champions at Nagano in 1998. More than 100,000 people gathered in the Old Town Square to give the players a hero's welcome on their return from Japan. It was a triumph for Jaromír Jágr and Dominik Hašek, the two most popular players in the team.

### JB Sport

Dlážděná, 3 (D1)
☎ 24 21 09 21
✆ 24 21 09 51
Open Mon.-Fri. 9am-6pm, Sat. 9am-1pm.

There are two sports shops in the same street, one of which sells only ice hockey equipment. You'll find every accessory imaginable, from sticks to skates, not forgetting the inevitable national team shirts - every supporter of the modern-day Czech heroes should have one.

### Dům sportu-Teta

Jungmannova, 28 (C2)
☎ 96 16 51 11
Open Mon.-Fri. 9.30am-7pm, Sat. 9.30am-4pm.

This shop sells equipment for all sports and carries some famous labels. Sale items are on the first floor, including sports shoes, Bauer roller skates (made in the Czech Republic but designed in Canada) and ski gear. This is sold out of season and includes equipment for downhill and cross-country. Take a look at the Franciscan garden from the window in the corridor above the camping section.

### Hockey World

U Výstaviště, 21 (not on map)
☎ 33 37 05 25
Open Mon.-Fri. 10am-6pm, Sat. 10am-2pm. In summer open noon-5pm except Sat.

This shop is strictly for those obsessed with the sport. Posters, cassettes and collectors cards for the various teams are sold here. If it isn't to do with hockey, it won't be here.

### Sun & Snow Shop

Francouzská, 3 (D3)
☎ 22 51 30 74
Open Mon.-Fri. 10am-6pm.

Only two topics of conversation are ever raised in this shop – snowboarding and skateboarding. Once you've made your choice of board, you can select

your outfit from a range of T-shirts, shorts, trousers and even swimming costumes.

## Trekking sport – Humi

Martinská, 2 (C2)
☎ 24 22 50 85
Open Mon.-Fri. 10am-6pm, Sat. 10am-1pm.

This small shop sells everything you need to go trekking, from sleeping bags to tent pegs. There's even an indoor climbing wall. The staff are friendly

and informative, and they'll advise you on the best places to go trekking in the Czech Republic.

## Kiwi

Jungmannova, 23 (C2)
☎ 24 94 84 55
📠 96 24 55 55
Open Mon.-Fri. 9am-6.30pm, Sat. 9am-2pm.

This is a great find for those interested in walking or mountain biking. You'll find the usual travel guides in different languages, touring and city maps, and more unusual and interesting maps on footpaths in the Czech Republic, France and Spain that are very reasonably priced. You might even be lucky enough to come across a map of the Battle of Normandy, if you're interested in historical detail.

## U Petra

Dlouhá, 3 (C1)
☎ 23 17 530
Open Mon.-Fri. 9am-6pm, Sat. 9am-1pm.

You can purchase bait, fishing rods or hooks from the huge

selection in this shop. Add a Czech touch to your fishing equipment.

## Association Club Sparta Praha

Betlémské nám. (C2)
☎ 20 57 03 23
Open Mon.-Thu. 10am-5pm, Fri. 10am-4pm.

Sparta is the Czech Republic's best football team. It has more titles than any other Czech club and its stadium in Letná has the most modern equipment. Fans come to matches in droves and shop here for their tickets, flags, scarves and shirts. It's a treasure trove of football paraphernalia.

# ANTIQUES

When you go looking for antiques, you'll have the choice of luxurious shops or more humble market stalls. There are some good bargains to be had, from the smallest trinket to a magnificent silver service, so spend time having a good look round and you're

likely to be well rewarded. The professionals are probably a few steps ahead of you, but there's a wide choice for all tastes and budgets.

## Alma
Valentinská, 7 (C1)
☎ 23 25 865
Open every day 10am-6pm.

Don't stop to look in the shop windows on the ground floor, but make your way instead to the basement, where you'll come across the most interesting items. There's a huge selection of tableware, glasses, porcelain, lace, antique fountain pens, jewellery from the 20s and 30s and hat pins. You'll find the odd kitsch painting, if that's what takes your fancy. Antique buying can be thirsty work, so pop into the wine bar for a glass of local wine. It's on the same floor and is open Mon.-Fri. 10am-6pm.

## Bric à Brac
Týnská, 7 (C1)
☎ 232 64 84
Open every day 10am-7pm.

This is a good example of a Prague bazar. Situated just behind the Týn church, it has a large selection of more unusual stock at a variety of prices. You'll find old jewellery, lamps, watches, pens, typewriters and cameras mixed up with posters and other old advertising material. Beware the prices – the shop is in the heart of the tourist area.

## Dorotheum
Ovocny trh 2 (near Estates Theatre, see map p. 58)
☎ 24 22 20 01
Open Mon.-Sat. 9.30am-7pm.

This company has existed in Vienna since 1707. Treasures include jewellery from the 20s, porcelain and crystal pieces, paintings and furniture are all on sale. You may well come across a delightful silver teapot or an Art Nouveau vase in molten glass, but don't expect to do any deals here.

## Rudolf Špičák
Ostrovní, 26 (C2)
☎ 29 79 19
Open every day 10am-5pm.

As you push open the door to this curious shop, breathe in the smell of tobacco coming from the bearded owner's pipe. You'll find everything you could possibly think of in this establishment, with its interesting mix of tableware, books, clothes and advertising posters. It's well worth a visit for its atmosphere and extraordinarily low prices.

## Dračka Milan

Vitězná, 16 (B2)
☎ 53 06 24
Open
Mon.-Fri.
10am-5pm,
Sat. 10am-
noon.

You
should
enjoy
rummaging
through the
collection of
pieces in this old
shop,
and you might
just find a
rare item.
There are
shelves,
cupboards, tableware, lamps,
glasses, metal boxes, old wooden
tools, kitchen equipment and
much more. Prices are
reasonable and it's an interesting
shop.

## Jan Pazdera

Vodičkova, 28 (C2)
☎ 24 21 61 97
Open Mon.-
Fri. 10am-
6pm, Sat.
10am-1pm.

This is the place
to come if you
are a keen
photographer.
Located
at the
start of
the 'ABC'
arcade on
Vodičkova Street,
this shop is
difficult to miss.
It has all
the latest
cameras
alongside old
models that
have seen lots
of action. You
may have to wait
a little while to be served,
but it's certainly worth it.

## Václav Matouš

Mikulandská , 10 (C2)
☎ 29 14 48
Open Mon.-Fri. 9am-noon,
2-6pm.

Travel back in time at this
antique shop, which specialises
in antique watches, clocks
and old alarm clocks. You
won't beat any
records on
prices (a
chronometer
costs around
Kč350, for
example),
but make
sure you look
at the superb
Omega
watches (from
Kč1,200-4,000)
and the fob watches
(from Kč900-4,000). Take time
out here.

## U sv. Martina

Martinská, 4
(C2)
☎ 26 65 15
Open Mon.-
Fri. 10am-
1pm, 2-6pm,
Sat. 10am-
2pm.

Not
everything in
this shop is
worth looking
at, but if you pass
quickly by the ceramic
trinkets, you can spend
more time admiring the

original wall-mounted
coffee grinders
(wooden ones start
at Kč2,500 and
ceramic ones at
Kč7,500). There are
also some lovely wooden
clocks (from Kč3,000).

## Useful words

It's important to understand
the different types of shops
you can look in when hunting
for antiques and secondhand
goods. All over Prague are
examples of the *bazar*, which
sell a mixture of secondhand
clothes, furniture and electrical
goods at bargain prices. The
*starožitnosti*, on the other hand,
is an antique shop, often a
specialist, in which quality items
are professionally displayed
and expensively priced. An
*antika* is an antique, but an
*antikvariát* is a secondhand
bookseller, who often has the
odd old book worth a second
look (see p. 102).

KÁVA

## SECONDHAND BOOKS

Secondhand books are often sold in very upmarket shops, and as much attention and shelf space is given to them as to new publications. Almost all booksellers have foreign language books (English-language bookstores are known as *knihkupectví* and are supported by the expatriate community). It's also worth searching for old maps, atlases, sketches, prints and postcards, many of which can be fascinating. You won't be able to go far in Prague without coming across a secondhand bookseller.

Nové schody zámecké.

### Antikvariát

Kaprova, 52/6 (C1)
(entry on Valentinská)
☎ 24 81 62 53
Open Mon.-Fri. 10am-6pm,
Sat. 10am-2pm.

There's an impressive selection of books and prints in this store, and many of them are worth a close look. The prints start at around Kč450, and the staff will be more than happy to take you through their collection, which is quite impressive.

### U Zlaté Číše

Nerudova, 16/212 (C1)
☎ 57 53 13 93
Open Mon.-Sat. 10am-6pm.

Among the timeless collection of postcards, engravings, old cinema magazines and literary works in Czech and German, you'll find a selection of fine art books, and several shelves devoted to inexpensive books. They even have a few old kitsch photos, too.

### Antikvariát Makovský & Gregor

Kaprova, 9 (C1)
☎ and 🖷 23 28 335
Open every day 9am-7pm.

This dusty old shop is piled to the ceiling with books on all subjects and in all languages (including Latin). You'll find good quality books at competitive prices, with the more expensive books carefully filed and stored in the back room. There's a selection of novels in English from as little as Kč30, as well as a collection of botanical and zoological prints and engravings from Kč1,500.

### Antikvariát

Široká, 7 (C1)
☎ 23 18 876
Open Mon.-Fri. 10am-6pm,
Sun. 10am-4pm.

A lovely scent of pipe tobacco greets you as you enter this shop, which is close to the Jewish quarter. At the back of the store are old photographs and postcards. There's also an international section, worth investigating for first editions. Have a good browse.

### Antikvariát Karel Křenek

Celetná, 31 (C1)
☎ 23 14 734
Open Mon.-Fri. 10am-6pm,
Sat. 10am-2pm.

Situated near the Municipal House, this shop is renowned for its high-quality secondhand and old books, particularly in German, and its old maps and prints of Prague. The prints and maps can be expensive, but it's worth having a good look round for books, as they can often be uncovered in the most unlikely places. They sell a handful of English titles, along with a few graphic and art books. Keep hunting – you might happen upon a rare volume.

### Antikvariát U Karlova mostu

Karlova, 2 (C1)
☎ 22 22 02 86
Open Mon.-Fri. 10am-6pm,
Sat. 11am-4pm.

A stone's throw from Charles Bridge is an absolute haven for lovers of rare books, old world maps and old prints (from Kč600-4,000). There are also foreign language books to hunt through. If you feel like spending an hour or so in a bookshop, then this is a good place to choose.

### Galerie Ztichlá Klika

Betlémská, 10-12 (C2)
☎ 22 22 05 60
Open Mon.-Fri. 10am-6pm.

There are two adjoining shops bearing the same name in this street. At no. 10, the gallery has an interesting selection of cards, sketches and prints (Kč300-3,000). At no. 12, you'll find yourself in book heaven,

surrounded by a huge collection of secondhand volumes.

### Terra incognita

Masná, 10 (C1)
☎ 23 28 697
Open Mon.-Fri. 9am-7pm,
Sat.-Sun. 10am-6pm.

The books in this shop are all very clearly categorised and arranged on the shelves, and the foreign language books are easy to find. There's a wide selection of literature and an impressive choice of poetry collections. Prices are very reasonable, and the books are generally in excellent condition. You can bring your own books here to sell, Mon.-Wed. 2-5.30pm.

# GIFTS, GADGETS AND UNUSUAL THINGS

There's really no limit to what you can buy in Prague, however out of the ordinary. For example, you'll have no difficulty finding fancy dress clothes, especially if you're in need of a cowboy outfit. You can buy magic potions, eco-friendly lotions and even a suit of armour. We've selected a few of the more interesting and unusual shops for you.

### Lucky Horse
**Karoliny Světlé, 9 (B2)**
☎ 24 23 47 29
**Open Mon.-Fri. 10am-6pm.**

Here's a little bit of the Wild West right in the middle of Bohemia. The 'John Wayne' look is very popular in Prague, and this is the place to come to find all the accessories you need to be a cowboy. Even the owner, Karel Hejtman, sports a cowboy hat and jacket and looks as is he's come straight from the distant plains. Felt hats (from Kč750), straw ones (from Kč290), oilskin coats (from Kč4,800), and even food for your horse are all on sale here. Whether you need a saddle or spurs, Karel will have them.

### Art Deco Gallery
**Michalská, 21 (C2)**
☎ 26 13 67
**Open Mon.-Fri. 2-7pm.**

This shop contains every imaginable Art Deco item from between the wars. There are pieces of furniture, necklaces, brooches, tea services, lamps, rings, glasses, decanters, paintings, ceramics and porcelain. The prices are relatively high, but it's an interesting collection, with some later pieces that are

round tins of tea and pretty bottles of flavoured vinegar, including such unusual varieties as orange and cardamom.

### Kondomerie

Karoliny Světlé, 9 (B2)
☎ 90 00 15 26
Open Mon.-Sat. 10am-7pm.

worth a look. Try and negotiate on the prices in English or German with Miroslava Vávrová, who tracked down all the items personally.

### Botanicus

Týnský dvůr čp., 1049 (C1)
☎ 24 89 54 46
Open every day 10am-9pm.

This shop is located in the beautiful Týn courtyard. Everything is natural and made according to traditional methods as practised

It appears from recent surveys that infidelity among Czech couples is quite common but the use of condoms less so. This shop aims to improve the latter situation and has fun condoms for sale, some of them quite unusual. Condoms that look like political figures (including Václav Havel and Václav Klaus) and monster lookalikes are among the more extraordinary designs. However, with prices starting at around Kč50 each, they're beyond the budget of most young people who one would imagine are the target market.

### Galerie U Rytíře Kryštofa

Kožná, 8 (C2)
☎ 24 23 63 00
Open every day 10am-7pm.

in Ostra, a 'green' village north of Prague. Great attention is paid to the packaging of the products, which turns a small purchase into a lovely gift. Choose from eucalyptus soap,

### Tatoo Pes Studio

Jilská, 22, first floor (C2)
☎ 24 23 57 66
Open Mon.-Sat. 11am-7pm, Sun. 1pm-6pm.

If you're feeling brave, climb the stairs at the end of the alleyway and you could soon find yourself equipped with a fashionable tattoo or body piercing (from Kč800). The more cowardly can settle for a suede jacket (from Kč500) and 'rave' glasses or yellow trousers with a contrasting pink nylon shirt. Stock up on CDs (techno, pop and rock) and hair dye. Back on the street you'll be able to get all the information you need on the trendy venues, where your new purchases can be shown off in all their glory.

The medieval theme is very popular in Prague, and can be seen at most village fêtes and fairs. On these occasions, tents are erected in the streets, and there are dances, sword fights, huge vats of soup and plenty of mead. In this shop you'll find armour, swords and sabres for enthusiasts, together with copies of models exhibited in Golden Lane (see p. 44). Wander around the shop to the melodious sound of medieval music, and you'll be transported back in time.

# SECONDHAND CLOTHES AND CDS

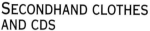

In Prague most secondhand clothes shops cater for the elderly or those on low incomes. The choice can be quite limited as a result, but this is gradually changing. If you're looking for clothes in particular, then only a few places are worth a visit. However, secondhand CDs are on sale everywhere, and you may well come across a few collector's items for around Kč350. It's certainly worth having a good look round.

### Mýrnyx týrnyx
Saská ulička (B1)
☎ 29 79 38
Open Mon.-Sun. 11am-7pm.

Close to Charles Bridge, this shop has a large selection of unusual and sometimes provocative dresses (from Kč350-5,000). They come in a variety of colours and a choice of mostly synthetic fabrics. There's a strong emphasis on fashions from the 70s and 80s.

### Second-Hand-Markt
Jungmannova 16,
Prague 1 (C2)
Open Mon.-Fri. 9am-6pm,
Sat. 9am-noon.

You'll find a jumble of secondhand clothes in this shop which occupies two levels. Not only jackets, skirts, dresses and shirts, but also bathrobes and swimsuits and a large quantity of scarves (Kč30) are on sale.

You pay at the cash desk in the entrance either by item (Kč30-500) or by weight, according to the type of clothes.

### Bazar CD
Jungmannova, 13 (C2)
☎ 24 94 85 65
Open Mon.-Fri. 9am-6pm.

You can't miss this shop. Just follow the arrows into the courtyard and to the end of the passage. It has a small selection of CDs, with a mixture of rock, pop, local and international music.

## Gung Ho CD Bazar

Rock Café
Národní, 20 (C2)
☎ 24 91 44 14
Open Mon.-Fri. 10am-11pm,
Sat. 8-11pm.

Only visit the Rock Café Club
downstairs if you're a fan of
hard rock, trash metal or heavy
metal – anyone else will be
disappointed. There are T-shirts,
video cassettes and even vinyl
records on sale.

## CD Bazar

Železná, 16 (C1)
☎ 24 22 65 90
Open Mon.-Fri. 10am-6pm,
Sat. noon-4pm.

This shop is located inside the
Železná Club. Cross the porch
and take the stairs leading down
to the basement. secondhand
CDs are on sale before, during
and after the concerts, at a very
small reduction. You'll find
mainly jazz, but also rock and
pop music.

with a strong emphasis on rock
'n' roll from the 50s and 60s and
its greatest American exponents,
as well as a selection of 70s rock
and some blues. A great place to
look for that rare Chuck Berry
or Led Zeppelin album.

## Bazar CD

Karoliny Světlé, 12 (B2)
☎ 24 23 34 67
Open Mon.-Fri. 10am-1pm,
1.30-7pm.

Rummage around among the
rock and pop CDs in this shop
by both local and international
artists (Kč250). The jazz, country
and classical music CDs (Kč90-
180) are in the back room. You'll
also find posters of American
rock stars and video cassettes.
Czech folk music is
well represented for
those interested in
learning more.

## Bazar

Prokopská, 3/625 (B2)
☎ 06 04 85 36 56
Open Mon.-Fri. 11am-6pm,
Sat. 1-6pm.

This is the place to come for
'oldies but goodies', or so say
the posters on the walls. New
and secondhand CDs are on sale,

## SENIOR BAZAR

Senovážné náměstí, 18
(D2)
☎ 24 23 50 68
Open Mon.-Fri. 9am-5pm.

This shop has a very discreet
exterior and can easily
be missed. Elderly ladies jostle
inside, looking for the
best bargains and
swap dresses
with each
other as
they advise
fellow
shoppers and
direct them
towards the
dressing rooms.
More and more
young people are
now coming here
to take advantage of
the unbeatable prices
for authentic 50s
raincoats and 70s
dresses. Good quality
leather handbags are also
for sale at excellent prices
(from Kč40), and there are
clothes for both men and
women. Note that the shop is
closed between 15 July and
15 August.

# GOURMET SPECIALITIES

The most renowned and enjoyed liquid speciality in Prague is beer. However, there are some other gastronomic surprises in store for you too, including sausages and salamis, cheeses and sweet pastries. You should also sample at least one of the fruit brandies for which Bohemia and Moravia are famous, including of course, the renowned *Slivovice*.

## c.e.l.l.a.r.i.u.s

Lucerna pasáž
Štěpánská, 61 (C2)
☎ 24 21 09 79
Open Mon.-Sat.
9.30am-9pm, Sun.
1-8pm.

As your eye travels along the wooden shelves in this shop you'll see local liqueurs, wine and other types of alcohol rubbing shoulders with bottles from all over the world. The Czech fruit brandies made by Jelinek are recognisable by their lovely hexagonal bottles. A bottle of Bohemian kirsch or apricot-based *Meruňkovice* will cost around Kč240.

## Lahůdky Zemark

Wenceslas Square, 50 (C2)
☎ 24 21 73 26
Open Mon.-Fri. 7am-7.30pm, Sat. 8.30am-4pm.

This delicatessen is very centrally located and sells alcohol, wine and Czech liqueurs alongside meats and cheeses. You'll find yourself tempted by the open sandwiches (*chlebíčky*), which you can eat standing up at high tables. *Slivovice*, a white plum brandy and a Moravian speciality, is sold here. Jelinek is the best brand to buy, and you can choose between a long slender bottle and a round one (Kč180-320), as shown above right.

## Lahůdky Zlatý Kříž

Jungmannova, 19 (C2)
☎ 24 94 68 77
Open Mon.-Fri. 7.30am-7pm, Sat. 9am-2pm.

*Becherovka* is a bitter-sweet, yellow herbal drink, which can be served as an aperitif, a liqueur or as a cocktail with the local *Beton* tonic. It comes in a green bottle with a yellow label and is made from herbs soaked in the curative thermal waters of the town of Karlovy Vary. It's reputed to help digestion, due to the powers of the water. There's only one way to find out if it works for you!

## Čerstvých uzenin

Wenceslas Square, 20 (C2)
Open Mon.-Fri. 7am-7pm, Sat.-Sun. 9am-7pm.

Czech sausages resemble salami, and you'll find the same brands in almost all the butcher's shops and delicatessens. They're also available in this shop, where long, flat game salamis (*salám lovecky*) hang from the ceiling. You can also buy garlic sausage in the shape of an enormous clove of garlic (*salám česneskový*).

## ABSINTHE, 75% ALCOHOL AND STILL LEGAL

The Czech Republic is one of the few countries where absinthe is still freely available. Van Gogh's favourite tipple is a very powerful substance, made from fermented wormwood and banned in France since 1915, accused of causing seizures and hallucinations in heavy drinkers. A nasty green liquid, you're strongly advised not to drink it neat. To make it remotely palatable, set light to a spoonful of sugar soaked in absinthe and then stir this into the drink. Add water and take great care. This isn't a drink to mess with. (Around Kč425 a 70cl bottle.)

## Kliment

Na Můstku, 8 (C2)
☎ 26 31 76
Open Mon.-Fri. 7.30am-7pm, Sat. 8am-6pm, Sun. 9am-6pm.

Between the smoked hams (Kč160 a kilo), meats, salamis and homemade dumplings (*knedlíky*), you'll find tins of Astrakhan, the Russian caviar.

Although not a Czech speciality, it's very good quality, but it is a little expensive (Kč550-2,300). If you find that the Czech dumplings are not your thing, then try the caviar. If the price puts you off there's a classic Czech snack-bar at the back of the shop where prices will do less damage to your budget.

## Cukrárna Simona

Wenceslas Square, 14 (C2)
☎ 24 22 75 35
Open Mon.-Fri. 9am-8pm, Sat. 10am-8pm, Sun. 10am-8pm.

This small confectioner's shop sells Czech spirits and liqueurs, a selection of chocolates and the famous pancakes from Karlovy Vary, the *Oplatky Kolonáda*, shown here. They're available in a variety of flavours, including nut and chocolate. You can buy them in tins (from Kč20) or from the street vendors in the main tourist areas, who serve them hot.

## Prodejna U Salvátora

Náprstkova, 2 (B2)
☎ 22 22 11 61
Open Mon.-Fri. 10am-6pm.

This little spice shop is situated not far from the Vltava river, and is reached down a little cobblestone alleyway. As soon as you open the door you're greeted by a wonderful smell of spices – basil, thyme, vanilla, aniseed and cinnamon. On one side there's a menu showing all the herbs and spices, with at least ten different types of pepper (Kč40 for the green variety). On the other side are descriptions of all the prepared mixtures (e.g. *gulasové* for goulash), which are sold in small paper packets at very low prices.

# Nightlife practicalities

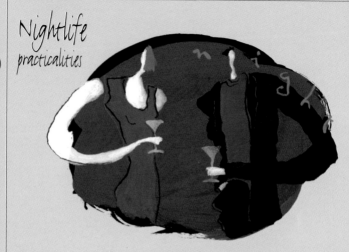

Night owls will enjoy Prague, with its wide choice of activities. Entry to most late-night venues is very reasonable. From enormous ballroom to intimate jazz club, from elegant opera to noisy disco, from Irish pub to Czech *hospoda*, Prague has it all.

## WHAT TIME DO PEOPLE GO OUT?

A night out in Prague starts quite early. The locals head for the restaurants at 7pm, which is also the time the curtain goes up at the opera. Jazz clubs warm up at around 9pm, but nightclubs don't really get going until 11pm and close their doors between 3 and 5am. You should note that events start on time in Prague, and doors close promptly. Be punctual when going to the opera, theatre or a concert, or you may find you're not allowed in. On the whole you'll find that the nightlife is relatively inexpensive.

## FINDING OUT WHAT'S ON

There are three publications that have all the listings you need. There is a monthly English publication called *Kulturní přehled* ('Culture in Prague') costing Kč40, which has information on dance, theatre, cinema, concerts, operas, festivals and galleries. There is also a weekly newspaper in English, 'The Prague Post', which costs Kč45 and features listings and cultural events and it's available from news-stands. *Do města* ('Down Town') is a bilingual weekly publication (published on a Thursday), in English and Czech, and is available from cafés, music

shops and information centres. It features not only cultural information, but is also vital for those interested in going to nightclubs and jazz clubs. Classical music concert programmes are usually displayed in church entrances. They're also distributed on the streets, in hotels and at the Prague Tourist Centre, located at Rytirska 12, Prague 1. Call ☎ 24 21 22 09 to book.

## WHERE IT ALL HAPPENS

Everything happens in the relatively small area between the New Town and the Old Town, which means you can enjoy a number of venues in one evening. Make sure you investigate the Malá Strana as well. When you cross Charles Bridge at night, you'll have a fantastic view of the Castle illuminated in all its splendour. (Street lighting is turned off at midnight.) Entry to the night-clubs isn't expensive and the drinks are equally reasonable.

## WHAT TO WEAR

A night out in Prague is an important event, and people dress up for the occasion. You shouldn't turn up at the Opera or theatre in casual clothes. There's no need to wear a long dress or dinner jacket, but it's important to look smart. Have a look round the stand-up buffet in the interval for a spot of interesting people-watching. If you're heading for a jazz club or nightclub you can be more relaxed about your attire. Jeans, leather, tattoos and body piercing are all widely sported.

## TRAVELLING AROUND THE CITY AT NIGHT

The metro operates from 5am to midnight, and many night trams run from midnight to 5am. They all pass by Lazarská and Spálená in the New Town and start with the number 5.

## TAXIS

Taxis are still good value but do take care as tourists are seen as easy prey. There are four basic rules to observe. Hail a cab rather than take one at a taxi rank, choose a basic Czech model of vehicle, such as a Škoda, sit in the front and try to negotiate a fare before setting off. The minimum charge is Kč25 and the price

per kilometre should be attached to the door (usually Kč17.50). Ask the driver to switch on the meter and ensure it's set at the correct rate for the city (it should be set at 1, the cheapest of the four rates). If you do have problems, ask for a receipt.

The following are reliable companies who speak English:

### Profitaxi
☎ 10 35/22 13 55 55

### AAA taxi
☎ 10 80/31 22 112

## SAFETY

Prague is a safe city, even night. Tourists are unlik encounter any animosity aggressive behaviour. Hov do be careful of pickpocket and around Wenceslas Squar and never be tempted to chan money on the black market. Don't wear your most valuable jewellery, and make sure you take care of your bag, rucksack, camera and video. Leave your passport at the hotel, unless changing money – you won't need it during the day.

## WHERE TO BUY TICKETS FOR SHOWS

You can buy tickets in advance from the box office at the venues themselves, in some hotels and from the following ticket agencies:

### Ticketpro
Lucerna Palace, Štěpánská, 61
Open Mon.-Fri. 9am-8pm,
Sat. noon-7pm.

Salvátorská, 10
Open Mon.-Fri. 9am-5pm
☎ 24 81 40 20
website: www.ticketpro.cz

Pražská Informační Služba
Na příkopě, 20
Open Mon.-Fri. 9am-7pm,
Sat.-Sun. 9am-5pm
☎ 26 40 20
website: www.prague-info.cz

**Bohemia Ticket International**
Na příkopě, 16
Open Mon.-Fri. 10am-7pm,
Sat. 10am-4pm,
Sun. 10am-3pm
☎ 24 21 50 31.

You can reserve tickets for all ephone until 8pm ). During the and certain may find events However, you can -by tickets on the office of the

sival begins every year on 12 May, the anniversary of Smetana's death. It ends three weeks later, on 2 June, with Beethoven's Ninth Symphony. Prague is in full musical swing during this period, with prestigious concerts and operas taking place, for which you must book well in advance. Hundreds of international musicians come to the city to take part. Traditionally, a procession leaves from Smetana's grave in Vyšehrad and heads to the Municipal House, where his most famous work, 'My Fatherland', is performed.

For further information, contact ☎ 53 02 93 or
🖂 53 60 40, Hellichova, 18.

# CLASSICAL MUSIC

Lovers of classical music will be spoilt for choice in Prague, where there's a large programme of concerts and operas every evening. The quality does vary, as it's bound to with such a quantity of performances. Some scenery and costumes can be quite daring, as *Don Giovanni* in a tracksuit has demonstrated. The tickets cost around Kč300 for the opera and Kč250-400 for concerts in churches. Tourists pay more than locals, but it's worth the difference to attend a performance in such lovely surroundings. You should be aware that some rather mediocre concerts are put on solely for tourists, and leaflets for these are often distributed in the streets. Private concerts are generally much more expensive but they aren't necessarily of higher quality.

## OPERA

### Prague State Opera (Státní opera Praha)

Wilsonova, 4 (D2)
☎ 24 22 76 93
Metro Muzeum
Performances Tue.-Sun. 7pm.
Box office open Mon.-Fri.
10am-5pm, Sat.-Sun. 2-5.30pm.
Stand-by tickets one hour ahead of performance.

This is Prague's largest theatre, which was opened in 1888, and

is a miniature version of the Vienna Opera House. It has a mostly international repertoire, with English subtitles.

### Estates Theatre (Stávovské divadlo)

Ovocný trh, 1 (C2)
☎ 24 21 50 01
Metro Můstek
Performances Mon.-Fri.
2pm and 7pm, Sat.-Sun. 7pm
Tickets from Kolowrat Palace, Ovocný trh, 6.

Mozart's operas are a permanent feature of the programme here (see p. 10), but make sure you

try to see a performance in the original language rather than in Czech.

### National Theatre (Národní divadlo)

Národní třída, 2 (C2)
☎ 24 91 34 37
Metro Národní třída
Performances Mon.-Fri.
7pm, Sat.-Sun. twice daily.
Tickets from Kolowrat Palace & Ostrovní, 1.
Open every day 10am-6pm.

This theatre puts on a wide variety of opera, ballet and plays, mostly, but not exclusively, Czech.

## CONCERT VENUES

### Municipal House (Obecní dům), Smetana Hall (Smetanova sin)

Nám. Republiky, 5 (C1)
☎ 22 00 21 11
Metro nám. Republiky.

Performances every day
7.30pm and 8pm
Tickets from box office,
open every day 10am-6pm.

Another opportunity to visit the
Municipal House, where the
Prague Symphony Orchestra
performs in one of the largest
venues in the city. There are 1,500
seats in the ornate hall, which has
sculptures and frescoes dedicated
to Czech composers.

## Dům U kamenného zvonu

(Also known as The House
at the Stone Bell)
Staroměstské nám., 13 (C1)
☎ 22 88 00 36
Metro Můstek
Performances every day at
7.30pm. Tickets from box
office or Ticketpro, every
day 10am-6pm.

Only chamber music is performed
in this Gothic 14th-century
building, and you'll be served a
glass of Czech champagne (*Sekt*).

## Rudolfinum

Alšovo nabř, 12 (see map
p. 46)
☎ 24 89 31 11
Metro Staroměstská
Tickets from ul Listopadu, 17.

Home to the very prestigious
České filharmonie, the Czech
Philharmonic orchestra (see
p. 11), which was founded in
1896. The Chamber Music
Orchestra also plays here.

## CHURCH VENUES

## Sv. Martin ve zdi

Martinská (C2)
Metro Národní třída
Tickets from box office or
Ticketpro.

At 5 and 7pm every day there
are performances by an entire
chamber orchestra or the organ
alone accompanied by a trumpet.
Baroque music and Czech
composers dominate the
programme. You can only visit
this church at concert times.
Translated, its name is Church
of St Martin-in-the-Walls.

## Sv. Mikuláš

Malostranské nám. (B1)
☎ 53 69 83
Trams 12, 22, Malostranské
nám. stop
Tickets from box office.

If you're passing this sumptuous
Baroque church at 5pm feel free
to enter and listen to a concert.
The acoustics are excellent.
Mozart played the St. Mikuláš
organ with its 2,500 pipes in 1787
and his *Requiem* was played
here 3 years after his death.

## Sv. Jakub

Malá Štupartská, 6 (C1)
Metro nám. Republiky
station.

This church is renowned for its
Baroque Christmas mass and is
a favourite venue for organ
recitals and other concerts. The
programme is displayed at the
entrance to the church, and
concerts start at 6pm. You can
buy tickets two hours ahead of
the performance.

A classical music concert in the Church of Sv Mikuláš (St Nicholas)

# JAZZ

The Americans introduced jazz to Prague after the First World War, and it has now become something of a tradition in the city. The New Orleans sound has been heard in the jazz clubs since the 50s. Today's talented musicians, among them Emil Vicklický and Karel Růžička, combine all the styles and have even made a name for themselves abroad. In Prague itself Emil and Karel are part of the fashionable club scene and play alongside international artists. Concerts usually start around 9pm, and the programmes are eclectic but mostly of excellent quality. Jazz lovers won't be disappointed.

## Agharta Jazz Centrum

**Krakovská, 5 (C2)**
☎ 22 21 12 75
**Metro Muzeum**
Open Mon.-Fri. 5pm-1am, Sat.-Sun. 7pm-1am.

This club was founded in 1911, and as the organiser of the international Prague Jazz Festival, it's generally considered to be the city's best jazz club and is certainly one of the most popular. Located in a small room in a side street near the top end of Wenceslas Square, it has a consistently good programme of local and international artists. Regular Czech performers include the Emil Viklický Quartet, the Gabriel Jonáš Session 90, Jiří Stívin and Karel Růžička & Friends. You can buy records and CDs produced under the Czech Arta label at the door. An Agharta T-shirt signed by Jiří Vortruba makes a perfect gift to take home. You can also take a meal in the café.

all that jazz of Prague...

Krakovská 5, PRAHA1
tel. 22 21 12 75

## Prague Jazz Festival

The annual international jazz festival takes place in October and attracts some big names. Since 1964, the Agharta and Lucerna clubs have welcomed such major artists as BB King, Chick Corea, The Brecker Brothers, Jan Garbarek, Wynton Marsalis, Maceo Parker and Pat Metheny. It's a good idea to reserve a table at Agharta or Ticketpro (see p. 110). Huge crowds are drawn to the clubs when the festival is on.

## Jazz Club Železná

**Železná, 16 (C2)**
☎ 24 23 96 97
**Metro Můstek**
Open every day 3pm-1am.

This inexpensive venue with a warm, welcoming atmosphere is centrally located in a cellar. Local bands play every evening and you can buy a selection of secondhand jazz CDs. There's a live cobra in the aquarium on the mezzanine, where you might want to retire for a drink after the concert.

## U Staré Paní

**Michalska, 9 (C2)**
☎ 26 72 67
**Metro Můstek**
Open every day 7pm-1am concerts 9pm-midnight.

It costs Kč160 to enter this club (Kč60 for students), which is beyond the budget of some locals. It does have an excellent programme of bands, however, and there's a decent jazz restaurant serving good food. The club is in the basement, and the restored building also contains a restaurant and hotel by the same name.

## U Malého Glena

**Karmelitská, 23 (B1)**
☎ 53 58 115
**Trams 12, 22, Malostranské nám. stop**
Open every day 10pm-3am.

Start your evening with a Tex-Mex meal in this atmospheric pub on the ground floor. After your meal, go downstairs into the basement, where the rather eclectic programme alternates between jazz on Saturdays and Sundays, acid jazz on Thursdays and blues or Latin American music on other days. Arrive early or book a table, as it's a small, popular venue.

a pretty courtyard adjoining Vodičkova. The music tends to be traditional, as does the menu. Enjoy your meal or sip on a cocktail as you listen to the music, which starts at 9pm. It's advisable to get there early to secure a table.

## Jazz Café c. 14

**Opatovická, 14 (C2)**
☎ 24 92 00 39
**Metro Národní třída**
**Open Mon.-Fri. 10am-11pm, Sat.-Sun. noon-11pm.**

There's a friendly, warm atmosphere in this jazz café with its posters of great jazz artists on the walls. It's rather unusually furnished with gaming tables from the 1950s alongside some antique sewing machines, and the venue also has somewhat subdued lighting, but nevertheless a certain charm. It's a great place for a rendezvous with a few friends to get in the right mood before a concert. You can enjoy a salad or indulge in a few canapés before the night really begins. The Jazz Café is a perfect venue to start your big night out in Prague.

## Reduta Jazz Club

**Národní, 20 (C2)**
☎ 24 91 22 46
**Metro Národní třída**
**Open every day 9pm-midnight.**

This is Prague's best-known jazz club, frequented mostly by tourists. Bill Clinton played his sax here in front of Havel in January 1994, and they still sell the CD of this big event. Tickets are on sale after 5pm in the week and after 6pm on Saturdays.

## Metropolitan Jazz Club

**Jungmannova, 14 (C2)**
☎ 24 94 77 77
**Metro Národní třída**
**Open Mon.-Fri. 11am-1am, Sat.-Sun. 7pm-1am.**

There are only five tables in this small jazz restaurant, located in

# BLACK LIGHT THEATRE AND PUPPETS

The first Pierrot was the creation of Jean-Baptiste Gaspard Deburau, the son of a Czech mother and a French father. Since Pierrot came to life in 1796, in Kolín in Bohemia, the art of the pantomime has become an important part of Czech cultural heritage. Today, the Ladislav Fialka troupe continues this tradition. The late Fialka was born in 1931 and was a real master of mime. His troupe tours the world with his imaginative creations. The Czech school of mime is constantly developing and embracing new techniques.

## BLACK LIGHT THEATRE
### Černé divadlo Jiřího Srnce
Lucerna Hall
Štěpánská, 61 (C2)
☎ 57 92 18 35/990 04 94 34
Performances every day 8pm
Tickets from Kč490
Booking at Lucerna box office Mon.-Sat. 5-8pm, or booking agents.

Created in 1961 by Jiří Srnec, this was the first Black Light theatre in the world. The actors are dressed all in black against a black backdrop, making them invisible when manipulating puppets or objects and thus able to perform their visual trickery. The troupe performs a spectacle of mime and Black Light theatre, and since its inception has been staging *Ahasver, legends of magical Prague*, a piece set in the time of Rudolph II in which Faust, the Rabbi Löw and the Golem are also involved.

## Černé divadlo Františka Kratochvíla – Divadlo Reduta
Národní, 20 (C2)
☎ 24 91 22 46/21 08 52 76 (booking)
Performances Wed.-Sun. 7.30pm
Tickets Kč350.

The programme here alternates between *Miss Sony*, a comical farce about love, and the famous *Anatomy of a Kiss*, a humorous and poetic depiction of the relationship between a man and a woman, in which a simple drawing becomes reality.

## All Colours Theatre
Rytířská, 31 (C2)
☎ 24 21 11 80 (booking)
Performances every day 8.30pm
Tickets Kč430
Box office open every day 10am-10pm.

The All Colours Theatre performs 3 shows with Black Light theatre, cinema, dance and musical comedy in an intentionally kitsch production. *The Magic Universe* is a journey into the depths of time,

while *Faust* tells the story of the man who made a pact with the devil. *Concert in Black Light* introduces variations on the works of Haydn, Mozart and Vranický.

## Divadlo Image – Classic Prague Club

Pařížská, 4 (C1)
☎ 23 29 191/23 14 448
Performances every day at 8pm
Tickets Kč350.

This Black Light theatre venue staging pantomime and modern dance attracts crowds of tourists due to its location a stone's throw from the Old Town Square.

## Ta Fantastika – Unitaria Palace

Karlova, 8 (C1)
☎ 24 23 27 11/24 22 90 78
Performances every day 9.30pm
Tickets Kč420.
Box office open every day
11am-9pm.

Enjoy a mixture of cartoons, puppet films, action and eroticism at this exciting Black Light theatre venue. *Gulliver* is an adaptation of the works of Jonathan Swift and Jack London. *Alice* could easily be entitled *Alice in the Land of Special Effects.*

### PUPPET THEATRE

Puppet theatre has a very long tradition at the heart of the country's culture (see p. 20) and it would be

a shame not to see a puppet show during your stay in Prague.

## Špejbl & Hurvínek Theatre (Divadlo Špejbla a Hurvínka)

Dejvická, 28 (not on map)
☎ 31 21 24 13/24 31 67 84
Metro Dejvická
Box office,
Wed.-Fri. 3-6pm,
Sat.-Sun. 1-5pm.

The most famous puppet show in the city, the story revolves around a narrow-minded father, Špejbl, and Hurvínek his reprobate son, who is an intellectual extrovert. These characters have been made famous by television cartoons and are responsible for breaking down the traditional barriers of children's puppet theatre. Enjoy the comic performance, and then go and

treat yourself to one of the puppets so that you'll never forget the event (see p. 96).

## Zázračné divadlo barokního světa

Celetná, 13 (C1)
☎ 232 25 36/232 34 29
Performances every day 8.30pm
Tickets Kč490.

The show draws on Prague's famous Baroque tradition for its choice of music and scenery, and marries it successfully with the ancient practices of opera. The skill of the actors and their interaction with the puppets is remarkable.

## Laterna Magika

Národní třída, 4 (C2)
☎ 24 91 41 29/22 22 20 41
Performances every day exc. Sun. 5pm and 8pm
Booking at box office,
Mon.-Fri. 10am-8pm,
Sat.-Sun. 3pm-8pm,
or at Ticketpro.

Laterna Magika (Magic Lantern) were the founders of multi-media theatre back in 1958, and their success has been huge ever since. They create a wonderful world of illusion and special effects.

# NIGHTCLUBS AND LIVE VENUES

## Malá Strana

### Jo's Bar

Malostranské nám., 7 (B1)
☎ 90 01 16 12
Trams 12, 22, Malostranské nám. stop
Open every day 11-5am.

This narrow American bar on the ground floor is always lively and serves good-value Tex-Mex food all day. The back room tends to be quieter.

### Jo's Garaz

Malostranské nám., 7 (B1)
☎ 90 01 16 12
Open every day 9pm-5am
Entry free.

Take the stairs to the right of the entrance to Jo's Bar, and you'll be able to dance the night away to pop music in the lovely vaulted basement. You may well be joined by lots of American students.

### La Habana

Míšeňská, 12 (B1)
☎ 57 31 51 04
Trams 12, 22, Malostranské nám. stop.
Open every day 5pm-3am
Entry free.

You can eat and drink upstairs in this Cuban bar, or do a spot of salsa dancing downstairs. When the dance schools arrive, it tends to get very lively on the dance floor, so those with two left feet beware!

### Malostranská Beseda

Malostranské nám., 21 (B1)
☎ 53 90 24
Trams 12, 22, Malostranské nám. stop
Open every day 11am-10pm.

MALOSTRANSKÁ BESEDA

MALOSTRANSKÁ BESEDA
MALOSTRANSKÁ BESEDA

MUSIC CLUB

Take the stairs to the first floor, where you'll find several local rock groups performing Czech-style 60s and 70s music in the small concert room. This venue has a real Czech flavour and an unusually minimal decor. However, there are often some interesting local paintings or photographs on the walls which liven up the scene. It's advisable to arrive early when the atmosphere is very lively.

### Rock Club Újezd

Újezd, 18 (B2)
☎ 25 05 08 18
Trams 12, 22, Újezd stop.
Open 11am-4am.

The first private club to open after the Velvet Revolution, today it's the favourite haunt of Prague's 'grunge' youth. On the ground floor there's a tiny space that doubles as nightclub and concert venue. On the first floor there's a smoky bar with very noisy music. The youth in this area aren't generally too active. They'll be munching on canapés and shouldn't be disturbed.

### Scarlett O'Hara's Irish Pub

Mostecká, 21 (B1)
☎ 53 47 93
Trams 12, 22, Malostranské nám. stop
Open every day noon-2am.

This is one of the many Irish pubs in Prague. It's tucked away in a small alley, accessible via the courtyard of the U Hradeb cinema, just past McDonald's. It has a cosy atmosphere, and it's a favourite haunt of Irish and Scottish expats who reminisce over a pint of Guinness or cider. Spend St Patrick's Day (17 May) here or at Molly Malone's (p. 119).

# Futurum

Zborovská 7, Prague 5 (B2)
☎ 57 32 85 71
Metro Anděl
Trams 4, 7, 10, 14
Open every day 8pm-3am.

This rather dreary former nightclub has had a complete makeover and it now attracts a young Czech clientele who go wild on Fridays at the 80s-90s nights, where they dance under a giant TV screen showing old video clips. The bar also hosts a variety of live bands.

## Staré Město

### Blatouch-Café Bar

Vězeňská, 4 (C1)
☎ 23 28 643
Metro Staroměstská
Open Mon.-Thu. 11am-midnight, Fri. 11am-2am, Sat.-Sun. 2pm-1am.

The Edward Hopper paintings on the walls add to the literary atmosphere of this bar, with its shelves full of Czech translations of foreign titles. You can enjoy an intimate conversation in the

friendly atmosphere while sipping a cocktail (alcoholic or non-alcoholic) and enjoying a salad or toasted sandwich.

### La Casa Blu

Kozí, 15 (C1)
☎ 24 81 82 70
Metro Staroměstská

Open every day 2pm-midnight.

La Casa Blu is wonderful on a cold winter's night in the city. With sombreros on the ochre walls and tequila or rum cocktails, this is a great place to come to listen to Latin American music. You can have a chat with the owner Pepi and you're sure to always get a friendly reception.

### Marquis de Sade

Templova, 8 (C1)
☎ 23 23 406
Metro Můstek or nám. Republiky
Open every day 11am-3am

This large bar, with its high ceilings, red walls and long tables, has little to do with the Marquis himself, but it draws a mostly expatriate crowd. It's a good place to start the evening, and the atmosphere is always lively. However, sometimes the quality of the food can be a little unreliable.

### Molly Malone's

U Obecního dvora, 4 (C1)
☎ 53 47 93
Metro Staroměstská

Open Sun.-Thu. noon-1am, Fri.-Sat. noon-2am.

Another Irish pub, with an open fire, draught Guinness and cider, hot food, Irish music, Irish staff, rickety tables and an eclectic decor. The dedicated beer and whisky drinkers stand at the bar, and there are small concerts from time to time. You'll feel as if you've discovered a little piece of Ireland, right in the heart of Bohemia.

### Roxy

Dlouhá, 33 (C1)
☎ 24 82 62 96
Metro nám. Republiky
Open Tues.-Fri. 9am-2.30am.
Bar open Mon.-Sat. noon-midnight,
Sun. 5pm-midnight.

Formerly a theatre, traces of which can still be seen on the dance floor. It is also thought to have been the site of the first public film show. Nowadays, Roxy is the scene of much musical and theatrical experimentation, and it's a must on the list of things to do at night in Prague. Enjoy a really delicious vegetarian couscous whilst listening to techno music.

*The Roxy nightclub*

### U Králé Jiřího

Liliova, 10 (C2)
☎ 22 22 17 07
Metro Národní třída
Open every day 10am-midnight.

Just next door to the James Joyce pub (Prague's first pub), head down the steps to the left. This *hospoda* is always very lively and seats are hard to find, but do try to squeeze in. Don't miss the cellar, in which you'll also find a fun atmosphere. The place is frequented by young Czechs and the watchful puppet hanging from the ceiling is long past being surprised at the number of beers consumed.

## Nové Město

### Fromin

Wenceslas Square, 21 (C2)
☎ 24 23 23 19
Metro Můstek or Muzeum
Open Mon.-Wed. 8.30am-1am, Thu. 8.30am-3am, Fri. 8.30am-5am, Sat. 11-5am, Sun. 11-1am.

This restaurant and nightclub is not very remarkable except for its spectacular view of Prague, Petřín Hill and the Castle. Visit in the early evening, take the lift up to the 6th floor and sit in the café, near the win-dows where you can enjoy an aper-itif. If it's

summer, sit on the terrace overlooking Wenceslas Square. Breakfast is served from 8.30am.

### Lucerna bar

Lucerna Palace
Vodičkova, 36 (C2)
☎ 24 21 71 08
Metro Můstek or Muzeum
Open every day 8pm-3am.

On Saturday nights there are 60s or 80s evenings at this bar, and the lively clientèle can be very exuberant. It's the biggest club in the city, and has a varied programme, so it's certainly worth a visit. You might even catch some great, live jazz performances

### Radost FX

Bělehradská, 120 (C3)
☎ 24 25 47 76
Metro IP Pavlova
Open every day 11am-5am.

The vegetarian restaurant on the ground floor serves food until 4am. Choose from generous dishes of pasta, lasagne and salads with a sweet vinaigrette dressing. A musician sometimes makes an appearance in one of the two lounge-style rooms behind the restaurant, one of which is non-smoking. There's a psychedelic decor in the basement, where techno music is played until 5am by tireless DJs. Those looking for a more sedate time can enjoy comfortable chairs and tasty snacks upstairs.

### U Sudu

Vodičkova, 10 (C2)
☎ 22 23 22 07
Metro Karlovo náměstí
Open Mon.-Fri. 11am-midnight, Sat.-Sun. 2pm-midnight.

There's a heady mix of wine and beer fumes in this bar, which has several basement rooms. It's an authentic *vinárna* and a favourite with young Czechs, who enjoy the dark rooms and loud rock music. In summer, a few

tables are set up outside. If you're here in the early Autumn try a glass of *burčák* (young wine) with a *chlebíčky* (fresh open sandwich), available any time.

## Žižkov

### Akropolis

Kubelíkova, 27 (not on map)
☎ 22 72 10 26
Metro Jiřího z Poděbrad
Open Mon.-Sat. 5.30pm-2am, Sun. 5.30pm-midnight.

This ground floor bar is on the corner of the street and it's always busy in the evening. Enjoy a selection of local and vegetarian dishes and admire the rather strange and surrealist sight of the aquarium, fully equipped with sand and a giant compass. Just to the right as you leave you'll find a former cinema in the basement that has been converted into a theatre. The programme is both varied and original, and includes plays and musical concerts.

# More handy words and phrases

Czech is not an easy language to get to grips with over a weekend, but Czechs really will appreciate it if you make an effort to speak their language, especially since you cannot assume that they will all speak English. So here are some handy words and expressions which may prove useful during your stay in Prague. You'll find a guide to pronunciation on the back flap of the cover (you will definitely need to refer to this!).

## TIMES

**Yesterday**
Včera
**Today**
Dnes
**Tomorrow**
Zítra
**(Last/this/next) week**
(Minulý/tento/příští) týden
**(Last/this/next) month**
(Minulý/tento/příští) měsíc
**Day**
Den
**Morning**
Ráno/dopoledne
**Afternoon**
Odpoledne
**Evening**
Večer
**Night**
Noc

## IN THE TOWN

**Slow/Quick**
Pomalý/Rychlý
**Near/Far**
Blízko/Daleko
**Here/There**
Tady/Tam
**Straight on**
Rovně
**To the right/To the left**
Doprava/Doleva
**At the end of**
Na konci
**Opposite**
Naproti
**Next to**
Vedle
**Outside/Inside**
Venku/Uvnitř

**Street**
Ulice
**River**
Řeka
**Bridge**
Most
**Theatre**
Divadlo
**Cinema**
Kino

## MAKING A PHONE CALL

**Could I make a reverse charge phone call?**
Mohu telefonovat na účet volaného?
**I will call back later**
Zavolám později

## GETTING AROUND

**Airport**
Letiště
**Taxi rank**
Stanoviště taxíků
**Car (by car)**
Auto (autem)
**Bike (by bike)**
Kolo (na kole)
**On foot**
Pěšky
**Seat reservation**
Místenka
**Sleeper**
Lůžko
**Platform**
Nástupiště
**Railway timetable**
Jízdní řád
**Express train**
Rychlík

**Left luggage**
Úschovna zavazadel
**Case**
Kufr
**Bag/handbag**
Taška/kabelka
**Free (unoccupied)**
Volný
**Reserved/booked**
Rezervovaný/Zadáno
**Return ticket**
Zpáteční jízdenka
**Terminus**
Konečná stanice
**'Next stop' (heard on trams)**
Příští zastávka
**I want to get off at**
Chci vystupovat na
**Change (eg from tram to metro)**
Přestupovat
**Car hire**
Půjčovna aut
**Where can I hire a car?**
Kde si mohu pronajmout auto?
**Petrol/gas**
Benzín
**Driver's licence**
Řidičský průkaz

## MONEY AND BANKING

**Exchange office**
Směnárna
**Cash dispensing machine**
Bankomat
**Travellers cheques**
Cestovní šeky
**Credit card**
Kreditní karta
**Banknotes**
Bankovky

Coins
Mince
Do you have small change?
Nemáte drobné?
Pay in cash
Platit hotově

## AT THE HOTEL
Dining room
Jídelna
Towel
Ručník
Soap
Mýdlo
Hot water
Teplá voda
Cold water
Studená voda

## IN THE RESTAURANT
Bon appetit
Dobrou chuť
Ready cooked meals
Hotová jídla
Meals cooked to order
Jídla na objednávku

## GENERAL
Bouillon
Vývar
Eggs
Vejce
Baked/roasted
Pečený
Grilled
Opékaný/grilovaný
Mashed
Kaše
Fried in breadcrumbs
Smažený
Smoked
Uzený
Curry
Kari
Rice
Rýže
Dumplings
Knedlíky
Pasta
Těstoviny
Sugar
Cukr

Bread roll
Houska
Savoury
Slaný
Sweet
Sladký

## MEAT
Meat
Maso
Without meat
Bez masa
Ham
Šunka
Bacon
Slanina
Veal
Telecí
Liver
Játra
Chop
Kotleta
Poultry
Drůbež
Goose
Husa

## FISH
Trout
Pstruh
Carp
Kapr
Salmon
Losos

## VEGETABLES
Vegetables
Zelenina
Portion of mixed veg
Zeleninová obloha
Potatoes
Brambory
Carrots
Mrkev
Cabbage
Zelí
Peas
Hrášek
Leek
Pórek
Cauliflower
Květák

Onions
Cibule
Garlic
Česnek
Mushrooms
Houby/žampiony
Tomatoes
Rajčata
Lettuce
Salát
Cucumber
Okurka
Potato salad
Bramborový salát

## SAUCES AND CONDIMENTS
Mustard
Hořčice
Tartare sauce
Tatarská omáčka
Cream
Smetana
Whipped cream
Šlehačka
Salt
Sůl
Pepper
Pepř

## FRUITS AND DESSERTS
Ice cream (sundae)
Zmrzlina (zmrzlinový pohár)
Crèpes
Palačinky
Fruit dumplings
Ovocné knedlíky
Cake
Dort
Fruit
Ovoce
Apple
Jablko
Orange
Pomeranč
Lemon
Citrón
Pear
Hruška
Banana
Banán
Pineapple
Ananas

Plum
Švestka
Apricot
Meruňka
Peach
Broskev
Strawberry
Jahody
Raspberry
Maliny
Bilberry
Borůvky
Cherries
Třešně

DRINKS
A glass of
Sklenice ...
Juice
Džus
Soda water
Sodovka
Mineral water
Minerálka
A white coffee please
Kávu s mlékem prosím
Without milk
Bez mléka
Viennese coffee
Vídeňská káva
(black grainy coffee, topped with
whipped cream)
Tea
Čaj
(usually served black with a
slice of lemon)
Tea with milk
Čaj s mlékem
Herbal tea
Bylinkový čaj
Fruit tea
Ovocný čaj
Fixed price menu
Standardní menu
Menu
Lístek
Dish of the day
Nabídka dne
Meal
Jídlo
Oil
Olej

SHOPPING
I'm looking for ...
Hledám ...
Bakery
Pekařství
Letter
Dopis
Postcard
Pohled
Stamp
Známka
Travel agency
Cestovní kancelář
Grocery
Potraviny
Delicatessen
Lahůdky
Paper goods shop
Papírnictví
Bookshop
Knihkupectví
Second-hand bookshop
Antikvariát
Glassware
Sklo
Barber
Holičství
Hairdresser
Kadeřnictví
Sale (discount)
Sleva
Shop
Obchod
Large/small
Velký/malý
Colour
Barva
Bag
Sáček
Book
Kniha
Cotton
Bavlna
Dress
Šaty
Fashion
Móda
Hat
Klobouk
Jacket
Krátky kabát

Leather
Kůže
Price
Cena
Shirt
Košile
Shoes
Obuv
Skirt
Sukně
Cloakroom
Šatna

MAKING A PURCHASE
Can I help you?
Máte přání?
I'm just looking thank you
Děkuji, podívám se
I would like ...
Chci koupit ...
Do you have it in another
colour?
Nemáte to v jiné barvě?
Do you have a smaller
(bigger) one?
Nemáte menší (větsí) velikost?
Could I try it on?
Mohu si to zkusit?
100g of cheese
Deset deka sýra (1 deka = 10g)
200g of ham
Dvacet deka šunky
Half a kilo of apples
Půl kila jablek
A kilo of potatoes
Kilo brambor
That's enough (sufficient)
To stačí
Could I have a bag please
Jednu tašku prosím

LOCAL VOCABULARY
Czech
Český
Bohemian
Čech
Moravian
Moravský
Of/from Prague
Pražský
Slovak
Slovenský

## ACCIDENTS AND ILLNESS

I don't feel well
Je mi špatně
I have a headache
Bolí mě hlava
I have diarrhoea
Mám průjem
Accident
Havárie
Help!
Pomoc!
Police
Policie
Police station
Policejní stanice
Call an ambulance
Zavolejte sanitku
Hospital
Nemocnice
Dentist
Zubař

## SIGNS AND NOTICES

No parking
Zákaz parkování
No smoking
Kouření zakázáno
Out of order
Mimo provoz
Sold out
Vyprodáno
Entrance/Exit
Vchod/Východ
Self service
Samoobsluha
Open
Otevřený
Closed
Zavřený
Prohibited
Zakázáno
WC
Toalety/Záchod
Gents
Muži/Páni
Ladies
Ženy/Dámy
Keep clear
Nechte volný průjezd

Beware
Pozor
No entry
Vstup zakázán

## COLOURS

Black
Černý
White
Bílý
Red
Červený
Blue
Modrý
Yellow
Žlutý
Pink
Růžový
Brown
Hnědý
Orange
Oranžový
Green
Zelený

## NUMBERS

One/First
Jeden/První
Two/Second
Dva/Druhý
Three/Third
Tři/Třetí
Four/Fourth
Čtyři/Čtvrtý
Five/Fifth
Pět/Pátý
Six/Sixth
Šest/Šestý
Seven/Seventh
Sedm/Sedmý
Eight/Eighth
Osm/Osmý
Nine/Ninth
Devět/Devátý
Ten/tenth
Deset/Desátý
Eleven
Jedenáct
Twelve
Dvanáct

Thirteen
Třináct
Fourteen
Čtrnáct
Fifteen
Patnáct
Sixteen
Šestnáct
Seventeen
Sedmnáct
Eighteen
Osmnáct
Nineteen
Devatenáct
Twenty
Dvacet
Thirty
Třicet
Forty
Čtyřicet
Fifty
Padesát
Sixty
Šedesát
Seventy
Sedmdesát
Eighty
Osmdesát
Ninety
Devadesát
One hundred
Sto
One thousand
Tisíc

## DAYS OF THE WEEK

Monday
Pondělí
Tuesday
Úterý
Wednesday
Středa
Thursday
Čtvrtek
Friday
Pátek
Saturday
Sobota
Sunday
Neděle

# Conversion tables for clothes shopping

## Women's sizes

### Shirts/dresses

| U.K | U.S.A | EUROPE |
|-----|-------|--------|
| 8 | 6 | 36 |
| 10 | 8 | 38 |
| 12 | 10 | 40 |
| 14 | 12 | 42 |
| 16 | 14 | 44 |
| 18 | 16 | 46 |

### Sweaters

| U.K | U.S.A | EUROPE |
|-----|-------|--------|
| 8 | 6 | 44 |
| 10 | 8 | 46 |
| 12 | 10 | 48 |
| 14 | 12 | 50 |
| 16 | 14 | 52 |

### Shoes

| U.K | U.S.A | EUROPE |
|-----|-------|--------|
| 3 | 5 | 36 |
| 4 | 6 | 37 |
| 5 | 7 | 38 |
| 6 | 8 | 39 |
| 7 | 9 | 40 |
| 8 | 10 | 41 |

## Men's sizes

### Shirts

| U.K | U.S.A | EUROPE |
|-----|-------|--------|
| 14 | 14 | 36 |
| $14^{1}/_{2}$ | $14^{1}/_{2}$ | 37 |
| 15 | 15 | 38 |
| $15^{1}/_{2}$ | $15^{1}/_{2}$ | 39 |
| 16 | 16 | 41 |
| $16^{1}/_{2}$ | $16^{1}/_{2}$ | 42 |
| 17 | 17 | 43 |
| $17^{1}/_{2}$ | $17^{1}/_{2}$ | 44 |
| 18 | 18 | 46 |

### Suits

| U.K | U.S.A | EUROPE |
|-----|-------|--------|
| 36 | 36 | 46 |
| 38 | 38 | 48 |
| 40 | 40 | 50 |
| 42 | 42 | 52 |
| 44 | 44 | 54 |
| 46 | 46 | 56 |

### Shoes

| U.K | U.S.A | EUROPE |
|-----|-------|--------|
| 6 | 8 | 39 |
| 7 | 9 | 40 |
| 8 | 10 | 41 |
| 9 | 10.5 | 42 |
| 10 | 11 | 43 |
| 11 | 12 | 44 |
| 12 | 13 | 45 |

### More useful conversions

| | | | |
|-----|-----|-----|-----|
| 1 centimetre | 0.39 inches | 1 inch | 2.54 centimetres |
| 1 metre | 1.09 yards | 1 yard | 0.91 metres |
| 1 kilometre | 0.62 miles | 1 mile | 1. 61 kilometres |
| 1 litre | 1.76 pints | 1 pint | 0.57 litres |
| 1 gram | 0.035 ounces | 1 ounce | 28.35 grams |
| 1 kilogram | 2.2 pounds | 1 pound | 0.45 kilograms |

## A

Accomodation (last minute): **67**
Airport to the city centre: **6-7**
Air travel: **4**
Alcohol: **24-25, 108-109**
Aleš, Mikuláš: **20, 21**
Antique Glass Gallery 'A': **60**
Antiques: **100-101**
Art Deco: **14, 15, 19**
Art Nouveau: **14, 15**
Authors: **16-17**

## B

Baba Villas: **15**
Banks: **33**
Baroque architecture: **12, 13**
Bars: **118-120**
Beer: **24, 25**
Belvedere: **45**
Bethlehem Chapel: **59**
Boats, Vltava river trips: **31**
Bohemia: **12, 18-20, 22-23**
Bookshops: **102-103**
Braun, Mathias: **13**
Brokof, Ferdinand: **13**
Budget: **8**

## C

Cafés: **35, 39, 41, 49, 53, 55, 76-77**
Cars: **30-31**
Castles:
  Prague Castle: **42-45**
  Vyšehrad: **15, 64-65**
Cathedral, St Vitus's: **42**
Cemeteries:
  Old Jewish: **38**
  Vyšehrad: **64**
Changing money: **33**
Charles Bridge (Karlův most): **13, 21, 46-47**
Churches:
  Loreto, the: **13, 34**
  Our Lady before Tyn: **62**
  St Cyril and St Methodius: **40**
  St Mary Victorious: **57**
  St Nicholas (Little Quarter): **13, 48**
  St Nicholas (Old Town): **13, 17, 63**
  St Peter and St Paul: **64**
  St Thomas: **48**
Climate: **4**
Coach travel: **5**
Concerts: **112-113**
*Conservatoire*: **10, 50**
Convents:
  St Agnes's: **39**
  St George's: **43**
Conversion tables: **125**
Crafts: **50, 96-97**
Credit cards: **81**
Crystal: **18-19, 90-91**
Cubism: **14, 15, 18**
Currency: **8**
Customs: **7, 81**
Czech Philharmonic Theatre: **11**

## D

Daliborka Tower: **44**
Dances: **26-27**
Department stores: **53, 94-95**
Dientzenhofer: **13, 48-49**
Dvořák, Antonín: **10-11**

## E

Embassies: **9, 33**

## F

Food and drink: **28-29, 76-77, 108-109** (*see also* Restaurants)
Formalities: **7**

## G

Gardens:
  Franciscan Garden: **54**
  Ledebour Garden: **49**
  Royal Garden: **44**
  South Gardens: **44**
  Vrtbov Garden: **57**
  Wallenstein: **50**
Garnets: **22-23, 90-91**
Getting around the city: **30-31**
Getting there: **4-6**
Gifts and gadgets: **104-105**
Glass: **18-19, 91**
Golden Lane: **44**

## H

Hašek, Jaroslav: **16-17**
Holidays, public: **7**
Hotels: **37, 51, 66, 68-71**
Houses:
  Cubist: **65**
  Faust: **41**
  'Fred and Ginger': **41**
  Lords of Kunstat: **59**
  Moser: **19**
  Praha and Topic: **54**
Hrabal, Bohumil: **16-17, 59**
Hradčany: **34-37**
Hunger Wall: **56**
Hurvínek (Špejbl &): **21**

## J

Janáček, Leos: **10**
Janák, Pavel: **15**
Jazz: **114-115**
Jewellery: **15, 18, 22-23, 90-91**
Jewish Town Hall: **39**
Josefov: **38-39**

## K

Kafka, Franz: **16-17, 55**
Kampa Island: **51**
Karlova: **58**
Karlovo náměstí (Charles Square): **40-41**
Karolinum: **60**
Klementinum: **12-13, 58**
*Knedliky* (dumplings): **28-29**

## L

Language: **9, 121**

Local time: **9**
Loreto (Loreta): **34**

## M

Malá Strana: **13, 48-51**
Malé náměstí: **63**
Malostranské náměstí: **48**
Maltézské náměstí (Maltese Square): **50**
Mánes Art Gallery: **47**
Map of Prague: **78-79**
Markets: **94-95**
Martinů, Bohuslav: **10**
Men's Fashion: **84-85**
Metro: **30, 31, 111**
Monastery, Strahov: **36**
Monument, Jan Hus: **62**
Mozart, Wolfgang Amadeus: **11, 21**
Mucha, Alfons: **14-15**
Municipal House: **61**
Museums:
  Czech Glass: **19**
  Decorative Arts: **19, 47, 81**
  Dvořák: **40**
  Jewish: **38**
  Mozart: **11**
  Mucha: **15**
  National: **53**
  Smetana: **47**
  Toy: **44**
Music: **10-11, 88-89, 107, 111, 112-113, 114-115**

## N

Na příkopé: **54**
Národní třída: **54**
Neo-Baroque design: **12-13**
Neruda, Jan: **26**
Nerudova: **13, 49**
New Town Hall: **40, 62**
Nightclubs: **118-120**
Nightlife (practicalities): **110-111**
Nové Město: **52-55**
Nový Svět: **37**

## O

Obecní Dům: **15, 27, 61**
Opening hours: **33, 80**
Opera: **53, 112**
Orchestra, Czech Philharmonic: **11**

## P

Palaces:
  Buquoy: **13, 50**
  Cernín: **36**
  Kinský: **17**
  Kunstat, Lords of: **59**
  Lucerna: **27, 55**
  Michna: **57**
  Royal: **43-45**
  Schwarzenberg: **35**
  Sternberg: **34**
  Wallenstein: **13, 48, 50**
  Žofín: **27, 47**

Pařížska: **39**
Petřín: **56**
Post offices: **32**
Powder Gate: **60**
Public holidays: **7**
Puppets: **20-21, 117**
Puppet theatres: **116-117**

**R**

Religious Services: **9**
Restaurants: **36, 44, 45, 47, 51, 66, 72-75**
Rudolfinum : **46**

**S**

Secession: **14-15**
Secondhand clothes: **106-107**
Shipping goods home: **81**
Shopping (practicalities): **80-81**
Short breaks: **5**
Šípek, Borek: **13**

Škupa, Josef: **21**
Smetana, Bedřich: **10-11, 26**
Spanish Hall: **43**
Špejbl (& Hurvínek): **21**
Sport: **98-99**
Spring Music Festival: **11, 111**
Stamps: **32**
Staré Město: **13, 58-61**
Staroměstské náměstí: **62-63**
Stationery: **92-93**
Statue of St Wenceslas: **52**

**T**

Taxis: **7, 11**
Telephones: **31-32**
Theatres: **5, 21, 54, 61, 116-117**
Tickets for shows): **111**
Tipping: **67**
Toilets and rest rooms: **33**
Tourist Information Offices: **33**

Toys: **86-87**
Trains: **5**
Trams: **30, 111**
Transport: **30-31, 111**
Turnov: **23**
Týn courtyard: **63**

**V**

Vegetarians: **67**
Vejvoda, Jaromír: **27**
Villa Amerika:**13**
Villa Bertramka: **11**
Vlatava river: **46**
Voltage: **9**
Vyšehrad: **15, 64-65**

**W**

Wenceslas Monument: **52**
Wenceslas Square: **52**
Women's Fashion: **35, 82-83**
Words and phrases: **121**

This guide was written by **Florence Lejeune** and **Carole Vantroys**
in collaboration with Ilona Chovancova and Geneviève Pons
Translated by **Jane Moseley**
Copy editor **Margaret Rocques**
Additional research, design and assistance: Vanessa Byrne,
Jenny Piening, Dave McCourt, Susie Lunt, Jane Eady and Christine Bell

We have done our best to ensure the accuracy of the information contained in this guide.
However, addresses, phone numbers, opening times etc. inevitably do change from time
to time, so if you find a discrepancy please do let us know. You can contact us at the
address below.

Hachette Travel Guides provide independent advice. The authors and compilers do not accept
any remuneration for the inclusion of any addresses in these guides.

Please note that we cannot accept any responsibility for any loss, injury or inconvenience
sustained by anyone as a result of any information or advice contained in this guide.

## Photo acknowledgements

*Inside pages*
**Éric Guillot** : pp. 2 (b.r.), 3 (b.r.), 11 (t.r.), 12 (c.l.), 14 (c.r., b.l.), 15 (b.r.), 18, 19 (t.l., c.r., b.r.), 20 (t.r., c.l.), 22 (b.),
23, 24 (t.r., c.r.), 25 (c.l., b.r.), 27 (b.l.), 28 (b.c., t.r.), 29 (c.l., b.r.), 30 (b.r.), 31, 32 (t.l., c.), 35 (t.l., b.r.), 36 (t.l., c.),
37, 39 (t.c., c., c.r., b.r.), 40, 41 (c., c.r., b.l., b.c.), 44, 45, (c.r., b.r.), 47, 49, 50 (htc., t.r., c., b.r.), 51 (t.c., c.r., b.l.), 54
(t.l., b.l.), 55 (t.c., c.r., b.l., b.r.), 56 (c.r.), 57, 58 (b.l.), 59, 60, 63 (t.r., b.r.), 64 (b.l.), 65 (t.l., t.r., b.l., b.r.), 68, 69, 70,
71 (t.l., b.l.), 72, 73, 74 (t.c.), 75 (t.c., t.l.), 76, 77 (t.l., b.r., c.), 82, 83, 84, 85, 86, 87, 88, 89, 90, 91, 92, 93, 94, 95, 96,
97, 98, 99, 100 (b.l., b.r., c.), 101, 102, 103, 104, 105, 106, 107, 108, 109, 112, 113 (t.l.), 115, 116, 117 (t.c., c.l.), 118,
119 (t.l., t.c., b.l., c.r.), 120; **Pawel Wysocki, Hémisphères** : pp. 2 (c.l.), 3 (t.r.), 10 (t.r., c.), 11 (b.l.), 12 (t.r., b.r.),
13 (c.,b.r.), 14 (t.l.), 15 (t.r., c.r.), 16 (t.r., c.r.), 17, 20 (b.r.), 21, 27 (t.r.), 34 (b.l.), 35 (c.r.), 36 (c.l., b.r.), 38
(b.c.), 39 (t.l., b.l.), 41 (t.l.), 42 (b.l.), 43 (t.r., c.l.), 45 (c.l.), 46 (b.l., b.r.), 48 (b.c.), 52 (b.l., b.r.), 53 (b.l., b.r.), 54 (c.r.),
55 (t.l.), 56 (b.l.), 61 (t.l., c.r.), 62, 63 (t.l.), 64 (c.r.), 74 (b.r.), 113 (b.r.), 117 (b.r.), 119 (b.r.); **Gil Giulio, Hémisphères** :
p. 28 (c.r.), 35 (b.l.), 50 (b.l.), 51 (b.l.), 53 (t.l.), 63 (b.l.); **Philippe Renault** : pp. 3 (c.l.), 13 (b.l.), 24 (b.r.), 27 (t.r.),
42 (b.r.), 43 (b.l.), 45 (t.l.), 58 (b.r.), 61 (b.r.), 65 (c.r.); **Ph. Guignard, Hémisphères** : p. 46 (c.).

*Cover*
**Éric Guillot** : t.r., b.l., b.r.; **Stock-Image** : c.r. (figure); **Stock Image, Hugo Sara** : t.c.; **Stock Image, Pacific
Productions** : b.c.; **Hémisphères, Gil Giulio** : c., c.r.; **Hémisphères, Pawel Wysocki** : c.l.; **Philippe Renault** : t.l.

*Back cover*
**Hémisphères, Gil Giulio** : b.c.; **Hémisphères, Pawel Wysocki** : t.r.; **Éric Guillot** : c. (violin); **Philippe Renault** : c.l.

**Illustrations:** Monique Prudent

**Cartography** © Hachette Tourisme

First published in the United Kingdom in 2000 by Hachette UK. Reprinted 2003

Distributed in the United States of America by Sterling Publishing Co., Inc.
387 Park Avenue South, New York, NY 10016-8810

A CIP catalogue for this book is available from the British Library

ISBN 184202 000 5

Hachette Travel Guides, c/o Philip's, 111 Salusbury Road, London NW6 6RG

Printed and Bound in Slovenia

# STAYING ON A LITTLE LONGER

If you're staying on and would like to try something new, the following pages give you a further choice of hotels, restaurants and bars, listed by district. Although you can just turn up at a restaurant and have a meal (except in the most prestigious establishments), don't forget to book your hotel several days in advance (see p. 68).

Enjoy your stay!

Please note that the prices given should serve as a guide only and are subject to change.

## Malá Strana

### Dum U Červeného Iva
Nerudova, 41, Prague 1
☎ 57 53 27 46
Tram 12, 22
Double room around
Kč5,000.
*This hotel opened in 1995 in the building in which the painter Petr Brandl was born. It's at the heart of the tourist district and is on the road that leads to the Castle.*

### Hotel Coubertin
Atletická, 4, Prague 6
☎ 33 35 31 09
Buses 143, 176
Double room Kč1,700.
*This hotel is attached to the south side of the Strahov stadium in the suburbs. There are 30 basic rooms at reasonable prices, and it's a good choice for those with a car.*

### Hotel Hoffmeister
Pod Bruskou 9, Prague 1,
☎ 51 01 71 11
Metro Malostranská
*Recently built by Adolf Hoffmeister's son, friend of Picasso and other French surrealist painters, this unique hotel comprises 43 bedrooms and a restaurant.*

### Hotel Pod Věží
Mostecka, 2, Prague 1
Trams 12, 22
Double room Kč6,100.
*This small luxury hotel in a 12th-century building is right by Charles Bridge. It has twelve comfortable rooms with every facility you could want.*

### The Charles
Josefská, 1, Prague 1
☎ 57 31 54 91
Trams 12, 22
Double room Kč3,500.
*This hotel is a stone's throw from Charles Bridge and has Baroque decor, painted ceiling beams and plenty of facilities.*

## Staré Město

### Hotel Casa Marcello
Rasnovka, 783, Prague 1
☎ 23 10 260
Metro Staroměstská or nám. Republiky
Double room Kč5,900.
*This hotel near St Agnes's Convent is housed in a medieval building thought to have been home to Italian aristocrats. There's a good Italian (naturally) restaurant on the ground floor, a café and a garden.*

### Hotel Central
Rybná, 8, Prague 1
☎ 24 81 20 41
Metro nám. Republiky
Double room Kč3,500.
*This hotel is centrally located and reasonably priced.*

### Hotel Paříž
U Obecního domu, 1,
Prague 1
☎ 24 22 21 51
Metro nám. Republiky
Double room Kč7,000.
*This Art Nouveau hotel is just next to the Municipal House and has 100 rooms plus a restaurant.*

### Hotel President
Nám. Curieových, 100,
Prague 1
☎ 231 48 12
Metro Staroměstská
Double room Kč7,500.
*Relax in the sauna, then enjoy a flutter in the casino of this hotel with a 70s interior and a wonderful view over the Vltava river, on whose banks it's situated.*

### Hotel U Zlatého stromu
Karlova, 6, Prague 1
Metro Staroměstská
☎ 22 22 04 41
Metro Staroměstská
Double room Kč4,190.
*This is a charming hotel housed in a 12th-century building, situated near Charles Bridge and right in the heart of Staré Město. The restaurant is open all day.*

### U Krále Karla
Úvoz, 4, Prague 1
☎ 53 88 05
Tram 22
Double room Kč5,400.
*Housed in a Renaissance building, this hotel is on the extension of Nerudova, south of the Loreto. It has a good view over Malá Strana.*

### U Staré pani
Michalská, 9, Prague 1
☎ 26 72 67
Metro Můstek
Double room Kč3,950,
high season.
*This hotel in a restored building in the heart of Staré Město has 18 clean, comfortable rooms. The jazz club in the basement is worth a visit.*

## Nové Město

### Ambassador, Zlatá Husa
Wenceslas Square, 5-7,
Prague 1
☎ 24 19 31 11
Metro Můstek
Double room around
Kč7,000.
*This large hotel is conveniently located in the centre of Wenceslas Square. The rooms are clean but not very stylish.*

### Atlantic
Na poříčí, 9/1074,
Prague 1
☎ 24 81 10 84
Metro nám. Republiky
Double room around
Kč3,500.
*Centrally located, this is a large hotel with a restaurant.*

### Hotel Meteor Plaza
Hybernská, 6, Prague 1
☎ 24 22 06 64
Metro nám. Republiky
Double room Kč6,000,
low season.
*There are 90 rooms in this hotel, which is near the Municipal House. The hotel was renovated in 1992 and there's a restaurant in the converted 16th-century cellar.*

### Esplanade
Washingtonova, 19,
Prague 1
☎ 24 21 17 15
Metro Muzeum
Double room Kč8,400.
*Located just off Wenceslas Square, this hotel has 74 rooms, a café, a restaurant, and some lovely Art Nouveau features.*

### Grand Hotel Bohemia Praha
Králodvorská 4, Prague 1
☎ 24 80 41 11
Metro nám. Republiky
Double room Kč13,500.

*Situated about five minutes walk from the bottom end of Wenceslas Square, this hotel specialises in conference accommodation. It has 78 spacious rooms with many facilities, including private fax machines.*

## Hotel Adria
Wenceslas Square, 26, Prague 1
☎ 21 08 11 11
Metro Můstek
Double room Kč6,000.
*Having been completely rebuilt, this hotel has 58 cheerful rooms, some suites and a studio. It's centrally located and has a restaurant, a bar and a booking service for concerts and plays.*

## Hotel Axa
Na Poříčí 40, Prague 1
☎ 24 81 25 80
Metro nám. Republiky
Double room Kc3,600.
*Very centrally located, this hotel has 130 comfortable rooms and a swimming pool in the basement.*

## Hotel Harmony
Na Poříčí, 31, Prague 1
☎ 232 00 16
Metro nám. Republiky
Double room Kč3,340.
*Built in 1930, the hotel's 60 rooms were renovated in 1992 and there are facilities for people with special needs.*

## Hotel Jalta
Wenceslas Square, 15, Prague 1
☎ 22 82 21 11
Metro Mustek or Muzeum
Double room Kc6,600.
*There are 89 rooms in this 50s hotel on Wenceslas Square. Some rooms have facilities for people with special needs and the restaurant is good.*

## Hotel Morán
Na Moráni, 15, Prague 2
☎ 24 91 52 08
Metro Charles Square
Double room Kč6,200.
*Centrally located with a calm and friendly atmosphere, this hotel serves very generous breakfasts and has lots of facilities.*

## Hotel Radisson SAS
Štěpánská, 40, Prague 1
☎ 96 22 61 52
Metro Můstek or Muzeum.
*Finally opened in 1998 after many years of construction, this large luxury hotel is in a great location.*

## Hotel Renaissance
V Celnici, 7, Prague 1
☎ 24 81 03 96
Metro nám. Republiky
Double room Kč6,800.
*This is a large modern hotel with 300 comfortable rooms in a central location. Recently built, the hotel is functional rather than atmospheric.*

## Palace Hotel Praha
Panská, 12, Prague 1
☎ 24 09 31 11
Metro Můstek
Double room Kč8,900.
*This hotel ideally located near Wenceslas Square is one of Prague's most luxurious hotels. The service is of excellent quality.*

### Vinohrady

## Don Giovanni
Vinohradská, 157a, Prague 3
☎ 67 03 11 11
Metro Želivského
Double room Kč5,800.
*This enormous hotel with a pink façade has been open since 1996. It has 400 rooms, a restaurant, a café and a gym and is 15 minutes to the city centre by train or tram.*

## Hotel Ametyst
Jana Masaryka, 11, Prague 2
☎ 24 25 41 85
Metro nám. Míru
Double room Kč4,500.
*This hotel run by an Australian has a welcoming sauna for the end of a busy day's shopping and sightseeing.*

## Hotel Sieber
Slezská, 55, Prague 3
☎ 24 25 00 25
Metro Jiřího z Poděbrad
Double room Kč4,180 inc. breakfast.
*This hotel is 15 minutes from the centre by train, but it has very comfortable luxury rooms and a restaurant on the ground floor.*

HOTELS

### City Petr Holubec
Belgická, 10, Prague 2
☎ 22 52 16 06
Metro Nám. Míru
Double room Kč2,200.
*This hotel with 19 rooms is in a quiet but quite central location.*

## Nový Svět

### Savoy
Keplerova, 6, Prague 1
☎ 24 30 24 30
Tram 22
Double room Kč7,700.
*Situated in the Novy Svet district near the Castle, this luxury hotel has recently been renovated and refurbished in the Art Nouveau style.*

## Žižkov

### Bílý lev
Cimburkova, 20, Prague 3
☎ 22 78 04 64
Tram 5, 9, 26
Double room Kč2,400.
*You can dine outside at this hotel in summer.*

### Hotel Dalimil
Prokopovo nám., 2/540, Prague 3
☎ 22 78 26 65
Tram 5, 9, 26
Double room Kč2,750.
*Located 10 minutes from the centre by tram, this hotel has tables in the garden for a relaxing drink.*

### Hotel Ostas
Orebitská 8, Prague 3
☎ 627 93 86
Tram 5, 9, 26
Double room Kč2,480.
*Entirely renovated, this Art Nouveau hotel has 33 rooms.*

## Further Afield

### Attic
Hanusova, 496/6, Prague 4
☎ 61 21 30 45
Metro Pankráci
Double room Kč2,300.
*This hotel has 24 rooms at reasonable prices and is situated 20 minutes by train from the centre.*

### Atrium-Hilton
Podbřežní, 1, Prague 8
☎ 24 84 11 11
Metro Florenci
Double room Kč8,820.

*French owned and designed, this hotel was completed in 1990 and has 788 rooms, three restaurants, two tennis courts, a conference room, a sauna, a solarium and a terrace. Bill Clinton hired the entire place in 1994.*

### Braník
Pikovická, 199, Prague 4
☎ 44 46 34 07
Tram 3, 17
Double room Kč2,500.
*This hotel is to the south of the city, close to the Vltava and thirty minutes by tram from the centre.*

### Brno
Thámova, 26, Prague 8
Metro Křižíkova
☎ 24 81 18 88
Double room Kč2,700.
*This enormous hotel is 10 minutes from the city centre by train and has little charm.*

### Carol
Kurta Konráda, 547/12, Prague 9
☎ 66 31 13 16
Double room Kč3,000.
*This hotel opened in 1993 and is 30 minutes from the centre by tram. It has 50 clean, comfortable but simple rooms, a smart restaurant and a bar.*

### Corinthia Panorama Hotel
Milevská, 7, Prague 4
☎ 61 16 11 11
Metro Pankráci
Double room Kč6,200.
*A large hotel boasting 427 rooms, 10 suites and one presidential suite, together with three restaurants, a café, a gym and a swimming pool.*

### Estec Czechoslovakia
Vaničková, 5, Block 5, Prague 6
☎ 52 73 44
Trams 8, 22
Double rooms from Kč1,500.
*This hotel has 620 rooms at reasonable prices and is near Strahov stadium.*

### Hotel Alta
Ortenovo nám., 22, Prague 7
☎ 800 252
Trams 12, 25
Double room Kč2,500-3,500.
*This hotel has 87 small but comfortable rooms.*

### Hotel Belveder
Milady Horákové, 19, Prague 7
☎ 20 10 61 11
Trams 1, 8, 25, 26
Double room around Kč3,350, according to season.
*This large hotel has 120 comfortable rooms, with facilities for people with special needs. It's situated in a lively area, with shops, restaurants and cafés.*

### Hotel Diplomat
Evropská, 15, Prague 6
☎ 24 39 41 11
Metro Dejvická
Double room Kč8,000.
*This luxury hotel is the closest to the airport and a 10-minute train journey from the city centre. It has 382 very comfortable rooms.*

### Hotel Esprit
Lihovarska, 1094-8, Prague 9
☎ 84 81 80 44
Trams 3, 5
Double room Kč2,795
*This hotel is 20 minutes from the centre by tram in an uninspiring area. Its rooms are simple but smart.*

### Hotel Forum
Kongresova, 1, Prague 4
☎ 61 19 12 18
Metro Vyšehrad
Double room Kč5,500-8,000.
*This hotel built in 1988 has 530 rooms, a lovely indoor swimming pool, a fitness centre and a restaurant.*

### Hotel Kinský Garden
Holečkova, 7, Prague 5
☎ 57 31 11 73
Trams 4, 7, 9
Double room Kč6,500.
*This hotel in the Smichov district has been open since 1997 and is part of the Italian Marco Polo group.*

## Hotel Obora

Libocká, 271/1, Prague 6
☎ 36 77 79
Trams 8, 22
Double room Kč1,950-
2,760.
*This hotel is 30 minutes by tram from the city centre in a lovely, peaceful setting on the edge of the Hvezda forest with authentic taverns close by.*

## Hotel Olšanská

Táboritská, 23, Prague 3
☎ 67 09 21 11
Tram 8
Double room Kč3,000.
*This building dating from the 50s is known for its sports facilities, including a swimming pool and fitness centre.*

## Holiday Inn

Koulova, 15, Prague 6
☎ 24 39 31 11
Metro Dejvická
Double room around
Kč7,500.
*This large, imposing hotel looks rather daunting but the spacious garden is lovely in summer.*

## Hotel Mövenpick

Mozartova, 261/1, Prague 5
☎ 57 15 11 11
Metro Anděl
Double room Kč7,000.
*This huge hotel complex is in the Smíchov district. Recently completed, it has 435 rooms, two restaurants connected by a funicular, and a conference centre.*

## Hotel Union Praha

Ostrčilovo, nám., 1
☎ 61 21 48 12
Trams 7, 18, 24.
Double room Kč3,380.
*There are 57 rooms in this Art Nouveau building in the heart of Vysehrad, with a restaurant and bar on the ground floor.*

## Hotel Vyšehrad

Marie Cibulkové, 29,
Prague 4
☎ 61 22 55 92
Metro Vyšehrad
Double room Kč3,500.
*This 19th-century hotel is comfortable and welcoming. It's 10 minutes from the metro and 15 minutes from the centre of town.*

## Petr

Drtinova, 17, Prague 5
☎ 57 31 40 68
Trams 6, 9, 12
Double room Kč2,600.
*This pleasant and newly refurbished hotel is at the foot of the Petřín Hill.*

## Splendide

Ovenecká, 33, Bubenec
☎ 33 37 59 40
Trams 2, 20, 26
Double room Kč2,490.
*This large and rather charmless hotel is situated in a pleasant part of town, by the Stromovka, Prague's largest public park. Gorbachev, among others, once stayed here.*

## U Blaženky

U Blaženky, 1, Prague 5
Metro Anděl
Trams 4, 7, 9.
Double room Kč3,200.
*Situated in Smíchov, this pension has 13 rooms and a restaurant on the terrace in summer.*

## Malá Strana

### Kampa Park
Na Kampě 8b, Prague 1
☎ 57 31 34 93
Trams 12, 22
Metro Malostranské nám.
Open every day 11.30-1am.
*This pink house is perfectly located on Kampa Island, with a view over the Vltava. It's a very popular restaurant and you have to book ahead. Fish dishes start at around Kč600, and there are tables outside in summer.*

### Bazar Méditerranée
Nerudova, 40, Prague 1
☎ 90 05 45 10
Open every day noon-1am.
*This is a huge restaurant with several rooms, some with balconies, where you'll be served Mediterranean food in a Mediterranean-style interior.*

### Bohemia Bagel
Újezd, 16, Prague 1
☎ 531 002
Trams 12, 22
Open Mon.-Fri. 7am-10pm, Sat.-Sun. 9am-10pm.
*Choose from a wide selection of flavours, including garlic, onion, sesame and raisin. Salads and quiches are also served.*

### Cantina
Újezd, 5/598, Prague 1
☎ 0603 477 422
Trams 12, 22
Open every day noon-11pm.
*Enjoy Mexican food at reasonable prices at this restaurant. Some will be disappointed with the rather gentle use of spices.*

### Resto Renthauz
Lorentská, 13, Prague 1
☎ 20 51 15 32
Open every day 11am-9pm.
*Visit this restaurant on a sunny day and enjoy lunch on the balcony overlooking Petřín Hill. Unfortunately, the views are more spectacular than the food.*

### U Kocoura
Nerudova, 2, Prague 1
☎ 57 53 01 07.
*The best Pilsner beer in the city awaits you in this tavern.*

### U Mecenáše
Malostranské nám., 10, Prague 1
☎ 57 53 16 31
Open every day noon-11.30pm.
*This restaurant is housed in a vaulted Gothic room. The menu features well-prepared Czech dishes, in particular flambéed duck and beef. A meal will cost around Kč800 per person.*

### U tří zlatých trojek
Tomašká, 6, Prague 1
☎ 530 126
Trams 12, 22, Malostranské nám. stop
Open every day 11am-midnight.
*In this Czech tavern, you'll be served traditional Czech dishes at around Kč80. The interior is entirely of wood, with polished wooden tables and chairs.*

### U Schnellů
Tomašká, 27/2, Prague 1
Open every day 11.30am-11pm.
*Traditional food is served in this restaurant with a slightly strange decor, including a bearskin on the wall.*

## Staré Město

### Cerberus
Soukenická, 19, Prague 1
☎ 231 09 85
Metro nám. Republiky
Open Mon.-Fri. 11am-11pm, Sat. 3pm-11pm.
*The restaurant serves both Czech and international dishes, with an emphasis on delicious pasta meals.*

### Govinda
Soukenická, 27, Prague 1
☎ 24 81 63 70
Metro nám. Republiky
Open Mon.-Sat. 11am-5pm.
*This self-service restaurant has organic Indian vegetarian food, which is delicious and very good value. There's a small tea-room on the ground floor.*

### Krušovická pivnice
Široká, 20, Prague 1
☎ 962 20 001
*This authentic hospoda serves delicious draught Krusovice beer and home-made (domaci) Slivovice. Traditional hot and cold Czech dishes are on the menu.*

### Amilcar
Elišky Krásnohorské, 11, Prague 1
☎ 232 95 22
Metro Staroměstská
Open Mon.-Sat. noon-3pm, Sun. 6pm-midnight.
*A selection of delicious couscous dishes is served here, with vegetarian options. Located right in the heart of Prague, it's a refreshing change from the traditional restaurants.*

### Modrá Zahrada**
Pařížská, 14, Prague 1
☎ 232 71 71
Metro Staroměstská
Open every day 11am-midnight.
Entry in Široká road
*This pizzeria is in the basement and is warm and welcoming. The pizzas are good and the mixed salads even better.*

### U Benedikta
Benedikta, 11, Prague 1
☎ 24 82 69 12.
*There's a restaurant in the basement and a café on the ground floor, serving good Czech food for around Kč200 per person.*

### U Medvídků
Na Perštýně, 7, Prague 1
☎ 24 21 19 16
Metro Národní třída
Open every day 11am-11.30pm.
*Draught Budvar is served in this very typical tavern.*

### U Golema
Maiselova, 8
☎ 232 81 65
Metro Staroměstská
Open Mon.-Sat. 11am-10pm.
*This restaurant is located in the Jewish Quarter and serves meat, fish and poultry dishes at around Kč500 per person.*

There's one dish called rabinova kapsa, meaning Rabbi's pocket and the restaurant's name means 'Golem's House'.

## U dvou koček

Uhelný trh, 10, Prague 1
☎ 24 22 99 82.
Plzen beer flows freely here, accompanied by traditional Czech dishes.

## U zelené žáby

U radnice, 8, Prague 1
☎ 24 22 81 33
Metro Staroměstská
Open every day 6pm-midnight.
This is Prague's oldest wine cellar, dating back to around 1400. Cold dishes cost around Kč100.

### Nové Město

## Jáma

V jámě, 7, Prague 1
☎ 24 22 23 83
Metro Můstek or Muzeum
Open every day 11am-1am.
You can choose between Czech specialities or Tex-Mex food in this bar and American restaurant. They also serve generous breakfasts at the weekends Rock n' roll music accompanies the meals.

## Klášterní vinárna

Národní, 8, Prague 1
☎ 29 05 96
Open every day noon-midnight.
Located in a former Ursuline convent, this restaurant serves Czech food and international dishes. It's a good place to go for a candlelit dinner before or after a show at the National Theatre nearby.

## Mayur**

Štěpánská 61, Prague 1
☎ 96 23 60 51
Metro Můstek or Muzeum
Open every day noon-11pm.
Although the service takes a while in this Indian restaurant, the dishes are well-prepared with all the traditional fliavours and spices of Indian cuisine (vegetarian dishes available).

## Nad Přístavem

Rašínovo nábřeží, 64, Prague 2
☎ 29 86 36
Metro Charles Square
Open every day noon-midnight.
This is a very pleasant fish restaurant on the quay, where an average meal will cost Kč300 per person.

## Na Poříčí

Na Poříčí, 20, Prague 1
☎ 24 81 13 63
Metro nám. Republiky
Open Mon.-Sat. 11am-11pm, Sun. noon-11pm.
This large restaurant is made up of part pub, part wine bar and part elegant dining area. The menu has Czech meals plus more exotic dishes at Kč200.

## Na Rybárně

Gorazdová, 17, Prague 2
☎ 24 91 88 85
Metro Charles Square
Open Mon.-Sat. noon-midnight, Sun. 5pm-midnight.
Václav Havel used to live near this fish restaurant with its nautical decor. It's still one of his favourite spots and he once brought the Rolling Stones here. Grilled or fried trout and carp are on offer, with steaks and Chinese food also available, all at around Kč400 per person.

## Pod Křídlem

Vovšovská 7, Prague 1
☎ 24 95 17 41
Open every day 11.30pm-midnight.
This is a popular venue after an evening at the National Theatre nearby, and both Czech and international dishes are on the menu at Kč600 per person.

## Pizza Coloseum **

Vodičkova, 32, Prague 1
☎ 24 21 49 14
Metro Můstek or Muzeum
Open Mon.-Sat. 11am-11.30pm, Sun. noon-11.30pm.
There are two rooms in the basement, but it's still advisable to book a table at this popular pizzeria. The

**RESTAURANTS**

menu also has salads, pasta and fish dishes, with a selection of delicious vegetables.

## Pizzeria Kmotra
V Jirchářích, 12, Prague 1
☎ 24 91 58 09
Metro Národní třída.
*This basement pizzeria is Prague's first and justifiably its most popular. If you don't make a booking, you'll almost certainly have to queue.*

## Rôtisserie Restaurant
Mikulanská, 6, Prague 1
☎ 24 91 45 57
Metro Národní třída
Open every day 11.30am-3.30pm, 5.30pm-midnight.
*Czech roast meat, poultry and fish dishes are on the menu here. Try the 'Old Bohemian' assortment, which gives you a generous selection of each.*

## Rusalka
Na Struze, 1, Prague 1
☎ 24 91 58 76
Metro Národní třída or Charles Square
Open Mon.-Fri. 11am-midnight, Sat.-Sun. noon-midnight.
*This little restaurant is just behind the National Theatre and can get very busy in the evening. A meal will cost Kč400 per person.*

## Šumava
Štěpánská 3, Prague 1
☎ 24 92 00 51
Open every day 9am-10pm.
*In this pleasant tavern the food is somewhat heavy but good nonetheless. There's a big room at the back, and they serve excellent Budvar de České Budejovice, which you can enjoy on the pavement terrace.*

## Thrakia**
Rubešova, 12, Prague 2
☎ 24 21 71 35
Metro Muzeum
Open every day 11am-11pm.
*This is a delicious Bulgarian restaurant, where you can discover Balkan delicacies. Try the fresh cucumber soup with yoghurt (tarator) and have a raki with your coffee.*

## U Fleků
Křemencova, 11, Prague 1
☎ 24 91 51 18
Metro Národní třída
Open every day 9am-11pm.
*This has become quite a tourist spot but is worth a detour, particularly in summer, when you can sit on the terrace outside. The rooms are large and the dark beer excellent, though you may have to grab a waiter to be served one. They also serve good Czech dishes.*

## U Supů
Spálená, 41/103, Prague 1
☎ 29 93 10
Metro Národní třída
Open Mon.-Sat. 10.30am-midnight, Sun. 1pm-midnight.
*This small restaurant is perfect for a quick dinner but the food can be heavy.*

## Universal
V Jirchářích, 6, Prague 1
☎ 24 91 81 82
Open every day 11.30-1am.
*This is a new restaurant decorated in 50s style serving excellent French bistrot food. The whole menu is delicious, from the salmon tartare and fillet of beef to the crème brûlée. A wide selection of dishes is on offer, at the very reasonable price of Kč150 per person.*

---
## Vinohrady
---

## Ambiente
Mánesova, 59, Prague 2
☎ 62 75 913
Metro Muzeum
Open Mon.-Fri. 11am-midnight, Sat.-Sun. 1pm-midnight.
*Tex-Mex food is served here, together with various American dishes, including spare ribs and pasta. The portions are generous and very tasty, and the decor has the theme of the American 'oil rush'. Bookings are essential, and there's also a second restaurant at Celetna 11, Prague 1 and a third at Ameriká 18, Prague 2.*

## Medůza
Belgická, 19, Prague 2
Metro nám. Míru.
*This is a relaxing venue, where you can order toasted sandwiches, salads, soups and Czech pancakes. Lights go out and candles are lit in the late evening, adding to the atmosphere.*

## Modrá Řeka
Mánesova, 13, Prague 2
☎ 22 25 16 01
Metro Muzeum
Open Mon.-Fri. 11am-11pm, Sat.-Sun. 1pm-11pm.
*This is a new restaurant serving Balkan specialities. The service is friendly and attentive, the decor warm and interesting, and the prices very reasonable.*

## U Hrocha
Slezská, 26, Prague 2
Metro nám. Míru
Open Mon.-Thu. 9.30am-11pm, Fri.-Sat. 10.30am-midnight, Sun. 11.30am-9pm.
*This local tavern has a friendly atmosphere and is a good place to come if you're feeling ravenous.*

---
## Further Afield
---

## La Crêperie
Janovského, 4, Prague 7
☎ 878 040
Open Mon.-Sat. 11am-11pm, Sun. 11am-10pm.
*This is the only crêperie in Prague, and it's actually French-run. They serve sweet and savoury pancakes, with honey, chestnuts, apples flambéed in Calvados, delicious cheeses and vegetables. The draught cider flows freely and the atmosphere is always warm and welcoming. It's a bit of Eastern France in the heart of Bohemia.*

# RESTAURANTS

## Malá Strana

### Café Savoy
Vítězná, 5, Prague 5
☎ 535 000
Trams 12, 22
Open every day 9am-10pm.
*This recently renovated 19th-century café has a high, gilded ceiling. Though it seems to have lost some of its former charm, it's still worth a visit.*

## Staré Město

### Baron
Pařížská, 24, Prague 1
☎ 232 92 21
Metro Staroměstská
Open Mon.-Fri. 8.30am-1am, Sat. 10am-2am.
*This is a very fashionable café, with framed photos of models on the walls, a glamorous clientele and cocktails on the menu. It's the place to be seen.*

### Chez Marcel
Haštalská, 12, Prague 1
☎ 23 15 676
Open every day 8-1am.
*This is a chic French café serving quiches, salads and other typical bistrot dishes. Relax with a pastis and a French magazine if you want to brush up your language skills.*

### Cafe Franz Kafka
Široká, 12/64
☎ 231 89 45
Metro Staroměstská
Open every day 10am-10pm.
*Located in the Jewish Quarter, this is a good spot to escape the stream of tourists. It's most relaxing in the second room at the back.*

### Jednorožec s harfou
Bartolomějská 13, Prague 1
☎ 24 23 08 01
Open Mon.-Fri. 11am-11pm, Sat.-Sun. 1-10pm.
*This unassuming gallery/café is a nice place to relax and write your postcards.*

### Gaspar Caspar
Celetná, 17, Prague 1
☎ 232 68 43
Open every day 9am-midnight.
*This café is attached to the Celetna theatre and is located on the first floor overlooking a pretty courtyard. English is spoken, since all the performances themselves are in English.*

### Gourmand au Gourmand
Dloua 10 37, Prague 1
☎ 23 29 060
Open Mon.-Fri. 9am-7pm, Sat.-Sun. 9am-6pm.
*A French patisserie offering a mouthwatering selection of quiches, sandwiches and pastries to take away or to eat in the attractive Art-Nouveau tiled interior. Only a short walk from the Old Town square.*

### Káva, Káva, Káva
Národní třída 37, Prague 1
☎ 26 84 09
Metro Národní třída
Open every day 7am-10pm.
*This café has a terrace overlooking a courtyard. Enjoy delicious carrot cake (Kč25) or tasty cheesecake (Kč45).*

### Terminal Bar
Soukenická, 6, Prague 1
☎ 21 87 11 11
Open Mon.-Fri. 9-2am, Sat. 10-2am, Sun. 10-1am.
*Surf the web at this trendy cybercafé for just Kč125 an hour.*

## Nové Město

### Café Archa
Na Poříčí, 26, Prague 1
Open Mon.-Fri. 9am-9pm, Sat. 10am-8pm, Sun. 1-8pm.
*Housed in the Archa theatre, this café is very relaxing in the afternoon but hots up before performances start in the evening.*

### Café Bar Tragédie
Lazarská, 7, Prague 1
☎ 24 22 89 80
Open Mon.-Sat. 11am-midnight, Sun. 3pm-midnight.
*A very tranquil theatre café. Come here for a relaxing afternoon coffee and read the Do Mesta (Down Town) magazine. You probably won't be able to find a seat just before a show though.*

### Café de l'Institute Français de Prague
Štěpánská, 35, Prague 1
Open Mon.-Fri. 9am-6pm.
*If you feel like a café crème and a Viennese pastry, this is the place to come. There's a lovely balcony for sunny days.*

### Růžová Čajovna
Růžová, 8, Prague 1
Open Mon.-Fri. 10am-9pm, Sat. 11am-10pm, Sun. 11-9pm.
*This tea-room is near Wenceslas Square but off the beaten track. They serve delicious biscuits to go with an impressive selection of teas.*

### Viola
Národní, 7, Prague 1
☎ 24 22 08 44
Metro Národní třída.
Open Mon.-Sat. 11.30am-midnight, Sun. 4pm-midnight.
*This café at the end of an alleyway was the favourite haunt of anti-establishment artists in the early 60s, and regular poetry readings and meetings are still held here.*

## Vinohrady

### Le Bistrot à vin
Polska, 2, Prague 2
Metro nám. Míru
Open Mon.-Sat. 11am-midnight.
*This French bistrot has an excellent wine list, and you can buy wine by the glass or bottle to enjoy with a plate of cheese or cooked meats. Have a look round the adjoining shop after your drink and choose some wines to take with you. Entry is via Anny Letenské street.*

# CAFÉS

# NOTES